D0558196

GEO-LOGIC

WITHDRAWN

JAN 2 4 2023

DAVID O. McKAY LIBRARY
BYU-IDAHO

PROPERTY OF
DAVID O. McKAY LIBRARY
BYU-IDAHO
REXBURG ID 8

JUL 2 9 2003

SUNY series in Environmental Philosophy and Ethics
J. Baird Callicott and John van Buren, Editors

JUN 2 4 2023

GEO-LOGIC

BREAKING GROUND BETWEEN
PHILOSOPHY AND THE EARTH SCIENCES

ROBERT FRODEMAN

STATE UNIVERSITY OF NEW YORK PRESS

Published by
State University of New York Press, Albany

© 2003 State University of New York

All rights reserved

Printed in the United States of America

No part of this book may be used or reproduced in any manner whatsoever
without written permission. No part of this book may be stored in a retrieval
system or transmitted in any form or by any means including electronic,
electrostatic, magnetic tape, mechanical, photocopying, recording, or
otherwise without the prior permission in writing of the publisher.

For information, address State University of New York Press,
90 State Street, Suite 700, Albany, N.Y., 12207

Production by Diane Ganeles
Marketing by Fran Keneston

Library of Congress Cataloging-in-Publication Data

Frodeman, Robert.
    Geo-logic : breaking ground between philosophy and the earth
sciences / Robert Frodeman.
        p. cm. — (SUNY series in environmental philosophy and ethics)
    Includes bibliographical references and index.
    ISBN 0-7914-5601-3 (acid-free paper) — ISBN 0-7914-5602-1
(pbk. : acid-free paper)
        1. Earth sciences—Philosophy. I. Title. II. Series.

QE6 .F76 2003
550'.1—dc21   2002030205

10 9 8 7 6 5 4 3 2 1

For De

CONTENTS

PREFACE

Geo-Logic is an essay in environmental philosophy. It approaches its subject through a curiously neglected field: the philosophy of geology. Philosophy and geology (or the Earth sciences) can each make crucial contributions to contemporary environmental concerns, but neither discipline will fulfill its potential until it refashions itself by engaging the other. *Geo-Logic* seeks to redraw the boundaries between the two fields, humanizing geology and bringing philosophy into the field.

I approach these issues from the perspective of training in both philosophy (a Ph.D.) and geology (a masters). This combination has also been leavened by experience in public policy. My time spent as a consultant with the U.S. Geological Survey has served as a check on both the conceptual rigor of my claims and their relevance to current debates concerning the role of science in society. Finally, my participation in a number of educational experiments (the Grand Canyon Semesters I & II; the Southwest Earth Studies Program; and currently, the Global Climate Change and Society Program, New Directions in the Earth Sciences and the Humanities, and the Flatirons Outdoor Classroom Project) has provided me with opportunities to test these ideas in the field.[1]

I have written *Geo-Logic* with four audiences in mind: the philosophic community; Earth scientists in academia and government; researchers and actors in political science and public policy; and interested members of the public. A central thesis of this work is that, in working on today's environmental problems, we must draw upon the combined skills of all these perspectives. *Geo-Logic* offers philosophers examples of how to relate environmental philosophy to science, public policy, and real-world problems. It shows earth/environmental scientists what is epistemologically distinctive about their work and how to respond to the cultural dynamics that are pulling them into the public sphere. It also suggests how workers in the public sphere can use the insights of the sciences and the humanities to better address the needs of communities. Finally, this book hopes to attract a readership among those members of the general public who are concerned with environmental matters. *Geo-Logic* thus continues the work in *Earth Matters* in seeking to create interdisciplinary communities for addressing our environmental problems.[2]

     Geo-Logic has a website: http://geologic.colorado.edu. The website has figures and photographs illustrating each of the chapters. It also has links to sites concerned with questions of environmental philosophy, the Earth sciences, science policy, and interdisciplinary approaches to knowledge. Throughout this book, citings marked "GL:CH1" refer to the website, where illustrations are organized on a chapter by chapter basis.

ACKNOWLEDGMENTS

Many have served as midwife to this essay: Tom Aldrich, Mark Bullock, Chris Buczinsky, Bruce Foltz, Trish Glazebrook, Irene Klaver, James Lough, Carl Mitcham, Jared Morrow, Dugald Owen, Dan Sarewitz, John Van Buren, and Win Wright. I also owe a debt to Chuck Barnes and Erle Kauffman (who instructed me in the art of reading rocks), and Al Lingis, Jim Marsh, Stanley Rosen, and Jack Zammito (who marked trails across the history of philosophy). The following institutions have offered support over the years: the Natural Resources Law Center at the University of Colorado; the U.S. Geological Survey; the University of Tennessee; and the Hennebach Professorship in the Humanities at the Colorado School of Mines. As always, none of the above should be held responsible for the opinions expressed herein. Thanks as well to my editor, Jane Bunker, who has skillfully guided this project to completion, and John Van Buren, whose sagacious advice helped me to draw together the threads of this argument. Finally, I have been sustained by the support of my family: Lee Frodeman, Barbara Frodeman, and Annie, Maya, and Denise.

1

INTRODUCTION

I.

I live in Colorado, in the shade of the Rocky Mountains, at a mile in elevation. And I sleep each night on an ancient ocean bottom. Six-foot-wide clams once filter-fed here; ammonites, curled in their spiral shells, sailed through the water column; and plesiosaurs, carnivorous underwater reptiles, paddled the murky depths of an inland ocean that extended from the Gulf of Mexico to the Arctic. Just south of here you can find ancient shorelines where dinosaurs traveled in herds: the sandstone ridges containing the footprints of their passage and the bones of their dead survive to tell the tale. Far to the west a string of volcanoes once rumbled: the ash from those eruptions turns our dirt roads into a tire-grabbing gumbo after a rain (GL:CH1).

Stand at the rim of the Grand Canyon and let your eye fall upon the Supai Formation, a brick-red, sparsely vegetated set of cliffs over five hundred feet thick. The Supai is made up of cross-bedded sandstones, red shales, and lenses of limestone. In the geologist's eye, these kiln-dry cliffs become near-shore mudflats baking under a tropical sun, crisscrossed by lazy, meandering rivers. Nor are such wonders limited to exotic locales. Go to Chicago and watch the Cubs play at Wrigley. While sitting in the bleachers, consider: eighteen thousand years ago what is now Wrigley Field lay beneath a sheet of ice two miles thick. This is geology—disciplined visions of past worlds drawn from the rocky palimpsest of the Earth.

This is also geology: not far from my home, in the offices of the United States Geological Survey in Lakewood, Colorado, teams of Earth scientists analyze data to help lawmakers and communities address questions of environmental policy. USGS scientists research the likelihood of natural hazards: when will the Mississippi River seek out a new channel, abandoning the port of New Orleans? How will the next major earthquake affect Los Angeles or the San Francisco Bay Area? Other scientists investigate energy or mineral resources, questions of water quality and quantity, and global climate change. Will declining mineral or energy reserves force the United States into questionable foreign policy decisions? How much longer will farmers in the High Plains be able to draw upon the Ogallala aquifer? This is geology in the public interest, traversing the boundaries between science and politics.

Finally, this too is geology: it is June 1997, the first summer of the Southwest Earth Studies Program. Ten undergraduates, half each in the sciences and the humanities, have come to study acid mine drainage in Colorado's San Juan Mountains. The drainage from abandoned mines is the American West's greatest single water quality problem. We attend a three-day conference on acid mine drainage that claims to make a special effort to speak to the concerns of local citizens. But the first two days of the conference are anything but community-oriented—we are inundated in graphs and statistics. Day 3, consisting of a field trip to old mine sites and damaged streams, consists of more of the same. We watch as the scientists place instruments into pools of rust-colored water, generating numbers expressed in obscure codes. The students look dubious. One turns to his friend and comments: "It just looks like sin up here."

Geopoetry, geopolitics, and geotheology are three loci of our relation to the Earth. Each of these sites disrupt the categories that have governed western culture since the birth of the modern age. Accepting the disciplinary boundaries of the academy, we proceed by ontological dogma—assuming that science, politics, economics, religion, and aesthetics are essentially discrete activities that can be examined in isolation from one another.[1]

The divergence between this parsing of knowledge and the challenges we face is becoming visible everywhere, but it is especially evident within geology. A complex set of forces—population growth, shifting cultural consciousness, advances in science and technology, and ever more pressing environmental issues—have made geology a prime site for the challenging of our accustomed categories of thought. Defying categories, geologic insights today often function simultaneously as scientific statements, political truths, and poetic and metaphysical incantations.

Geo-Logic explores this disruption of the categories of our intellectual and institutional lives. It is an ontological investigation with practical import. The problems facing society today require us to question the intellectual taxonomy that has trained us to think ever more deeply within the same old ruts. Reordering the categories of our thinking and our institutions—even more, learning to think across categories—will help us create new conceptual and social spaces for addressing our environmental challenges.

Consider the term "geology." Once identified exclusively with the study of the solid Earth, the term today has lost ground to "Earth sciences." The latter expression is meant to highlight the need for an integrated study of air, water, soil, rock, ice, and biota. Of course, few researchers in the Earth sciences address all of these concerns, but they all understand that the logic of their research requires them to go beyond the study of the solid Earth. Whether we are speaking of carbon cycles or the health of an estuary, the environment is an interrelated whole whose processes flow across disciplinary boundaries. Life becomes lithic (e.g., limestone), while tectonics influences patterns of evolution. To put the point differently, the terms "Earth sciences" and "environmental sciences" today represent a distinction without a difference. The fields have grown together—even if the former term still carries the tinge of its historical focus on resource exploitation. Our understanding of the Earth must be holistic across both space and time.

Clearly we must welcome this new, larger, Earth-scientific sense of the discipline; but we should hold on to, rather than discard, the older term. For "geology" remains the more fundamental expression. Our relationship to the Earth cannot be encompassed by science alone: "geology" opens up possibilities that an exclusively scientific approach to the Earth closes off. In ancient Greek, *Gé* or *Gaia* evoked the rich, earthy soil that sustains life; Mother Earth, the sheltering source and tomb of life; and one's *patria* or homeland. Our environmental questions require an account of the Earth that acknowledges all of these dimensions, an integrated *logos* of *Gaia,* an account of the planet that is our home.[2]

The meaning of the three terms introduced above—geopoetry, geopolitics, and geotheology—will become clearer as the argument proceeds; but perhaps some confusion will be avoided if I offer a brief account here. "Geopoetry" underscores the claim that the reasoning process within field sciences like geology shares as many characteristics with the humanities as with the laboratory sciences.[3] Geologists are poet semioticians, treating rock formations as stony verse, conjuring past worlds from the layers of an outcrop.

By "geopolitics" I do not mean the fact that politics have become international in scope, but rather that geology today lies at the center of political concerns, whether the issue is climate change, endangered species, natural resources, or the siting of roads and landfills. In response, Earth scientists are being drawn into new social roles. Unsettling our traditional understanding of their responsibilities, scientists must develop skillful means for navigating the realms of politics and culture.

And by "geotheology" I wish to emphasize that while environmental ethics has dominated discussions of environmental value, our relation to the Earth involves much more than questions of rights and obligations. Our response to nature includes the recognition that nature makes claims upon *us*. Our attraction to nature is in many cases grounded in a sense of awe and reverence before the tremendous forces and mysterious processes that have formed our world. If we wish to fully describe our interests concerning nature, we must retrieve the marginalized language of metaphysics and theology.

The Earth supports and sustains us, nourishes our children, receives our dead, and is the source of all our productions. Understanding our relationship to the Earth in all its facets is one of humanity's most basic challenges. Used in this more original sense, geology belongs as much to culture as to nature, and should be as deeply rooted in the humanities and in our public lives as in the sciences. To effectively grapple with our environmental challenges we must cross the boundaries that have separated the humanistic and scientific parts of geology; for while scientific facts concerning the state of our environment are crucial, facts alone cannot motivate the cultural changes that need to occur. Our environmental crises are fundamentally philosophical and spiritual in nature, and are more likely to be exacerbated than cured through the exclusive pursuit of Earth "science." Reordering geology in these ways will help us create the social and political spaces where researchers and the larger community can come together to address the future habitability of our planet.

II.

Geo-Logic does not only aim to redefine the conceptual space of the Earth sciences. This argument also seeks to redirect the humanities by bringing philosophy and the humanities into the field.

To see the opportunity facing us, consider Kai N. Lee's *Compass and Gyroscope*.[4] Lee is concerned with helping society develop the skills and institutions needed to reconcile economic growth, environmental justice, and ecological sustainability. Framing his discussion in terms of the close of the age of Columbus and the recognition of natural limits to society's activities, Lee's argument relies upon the metaphors of compass and gyroscope. His compass highlights the role of the sciences in providing us with reliable knowledge about the environmental effects of public policy decisions. His gyroscope emphasizes how democratic institutions stabilize society by limiting conflicts within the confines of open political debate. For Lee, the compass of science and the gyroscope of democratic debate are the two navigational aids we need to chart an environmentally sustainable future.

We must, however, add a missing third term to this debate—philosophy, or more generally, the disciplines of the humanities.[5] Lee rightly emphasizes the fundamental roles of science and democratic debate in mapping a sustainable future. But without the decisive contributions of the humanities our other efforts will be abortive. We can see why by revisiting Lee's metaphors. A compass can provide us with a sense of orientation; but it cannot tell us what our direction should be. Similarly, for open political debate to create the gyroscopic balance needed for societal stability, it must be supplemented by the inculcation of public virtues. The humanities provide a context for understanding the facts of science, and order and deepen public conversation through their hard-won wisdom.

The humanities make—or at least, *could* make—decisive contributions to both science and society. Scientists do science; it is not the task of scientists—at least, it is not their primary responsibility—to provide an epistemological and political analysis of what they have uncovered, or an account of the metaphysical implications of their work. Understanding how lab results or computer models play out in the endlessly complex, open-ended world we live in is (or should be) the work of philosophers, historians, and social critics. Philosophy in particular is well suited for uniting the insights of science with economic, political, ethical, aesthetic, and religious perspectives.

A similar point applies to the gyroscope of political debate. A stable democracy requires a populace that is educated in democratic virtues—open-mindedness, respect for evidential reasoning, and a commitment to pluralism—and that appreciates the metaphysical intuitions of different individuals. Statecraft requires soulscraft: the traditional concern of the humanities with the cultivation of the soul—what the Germans call *Bildung*, the moral and

aesthetic instruction that forms the basis of a mature individual—
is essential for tempering political debates. The point of public discourse is not merely to proclaim one's views, but rather to
understand and be educated by the views of others. The ancients
understood this conversational give-and-take, based in a common
commitment to fair, free-spirited dialogue, as one of the central
ways that rationality expresses itself in our lives.

Some will suggest that the roles I give to the humanities have
already been assigned—to the social sciences. The social sciences
contribute a great deal to society, and to environmental questions in
particular, but the substitution of the social sciences for what are essentially humanistic concerns has also caused much mischief. As the
name implies, the social sciences are based upon the assumption
that we can take a "scientific"—that is, an objective, value-free, and
quantitative—approach to human affairs. And indeed we can. But
doing so to the point of excluding the approaches of the humanities
impoverishes both our personal and political lives. The social sciences view values in the same way that economics treats consumer
preferences: as brute facts to be described, but not to be evaluated in
terms of their worthiness, or as liable to reformation through *Bildung*. But this dodges the essential point: some values are better
than others.[6] The upshot is that the social sciences have taught us to
treat our metaphysical, aesthetic, and theological concerns as curious cultural artifacts rather than as possibly true accounts of reality.

For an example of the contribution that the humanities can
make to society—and of the remarkable ways that geology and philosophy can play off of one another—consider Stephen Pyne's *How
the Canyon Became Grand*. Pyne recounts how Western culture either ignored the Grand Canyon, or saw it as a monstrosity, for hundreds of years after its discovery. Appreciation of the Grand Canyon
emerged from the confluence of two nineteenth-century streams of
thought: the nascent science of geology and the aesthetics of the sub-
lime. Moreover, Pyne notes that the creation of a geophilosophy was
the work of members of the intelligentsia—polymaths such as
Clarence Dutton, who married geology, aesthetics, and natural philosophy in order to portray the wonders of the West, and John Wesley Powell, who understood that geology and politics must be
combined if democracy was to flourish west of the one-hundredth
meridian. Taking works such as the paintings of Thomas Moran to
heart, American culture awakened to a unique natural landscape.[7]

Lee's appeal to compass and gyroscope expresses the modern
presumption that the solution to our problems lies in our devising

ever more artful tools. But rather than more instruments, the challenges we face require reflection and a patient commitment to conversation. Science concerns itself with facts rather than meanings; and (despite the libertarian biases of our culture) democratic debate must be tempered by the wisdom embodied within the humanities. We will grapple effectively with the challenges we face—environmental or otherwise—only by marrying the wisdom of the humanities to the insights of science and the deliberations of democratic debate.

III.

As they are currently constituted, the humanities are ill-prepared to play a substantial role in society. A passage at the beginning of Kant's *Grounding for the Metaphysics of Morals* (1785) puts the problem in a historical light:

> All industries, crafts, and arts have gained by the division of labor, viz., one man does not do everything, but each confines himself to a certain kind of work that is distinguished from all other kinds by the treatment it requires, so that the work may be done with the highest perfection and the greatest ease. Where work is not so distinguished and divided, where everyone is a jack of all trades, there industry remains sunk in the greatest barbarism. Whether or not pure philosophy in all its parts requires its own special man might well be in itself a subject worthy of consideration. Would not the whole of this learned industry be better off if those who are accustomed, as the public taste demands, to purvey a mixture of the empirical and the rational in all sorts of proportions unknown even to themselves and who style themselves independent thinkers, while giving the name of hair-splitters to those who apply themselves to the purely rational part, were to be given warning about pursuing simultaneously two jobs which are quite different in their technique, and each of which perhaps requires a special talent that when combined with the other talent produces nothing but bungling?[8]

Kant expresses the vision that has dominated our intellectual labors since the mid-nineteenth century: Knowledge, including philosophic and humanistic knowledge, consists of a series of domains best left to specialists. Kant accomplished this shift in philosophy via his "transcendental turn": rather than striving to identify the good, the true, and the beautiful, philosophy would now focus on the *conditions of the possibility* of moral, epistemological, or aesthetic claims. Thus in the *Grundlegung,* Kant did not investigate whether a given act was moral, but rather sought to identify the proper criteria for moral judgments overall (i.e., the "categorical imperative"). Rather than a reflection upon the nature of the good life, philosophy became professionalized, a domain governed by experts divorced from public discourse.

This attitude has resulted in whole series of research programs that have been in many ways quite remarkable. But it has also created the current chasms between humanities and society at large. As a consequence, society has lost the very vocabulary for making reasoned judgments about the good, the true, and the beautiful. Moreover, specialization within the humanities has led to systematic intellectual incoherence: lacking anyone tasked with offering a vision of the whole, we are left with experts unable to communicate with one another, or to frame their insights in ways pertinent to the public.

The aping of scientific methodology by the humanities has been a critical error. The analytic research project of breaking everything down to its smallest part, while reasonable within the sciences, has been toxic within the humanities. In form, the expectations surrounding a Ph.D. in philosophy today are no different from those in the sciences: a narrow investigation adding another diminutive brick to the tower forming the Babel of Knowledge. Such specialization contradicts the spirit of the humanities, disciplines that by their very nature are synoptic and global in scope. There will always be room within the humanities for the specialist's monograph; but the heart of the humanities lies in the work of the inspired generalist who labors to make a useful synopsis of issues of broad concern.[9]

How are philosophy and the humanities linked to the lives of our communities? Educators in business, engineering, and the sciences all have ready answers to the question of societal relevance, but the humanities rely on repeating traditional justifications of their place in the world. Humanists often reply with a question, asking whether everything in life must have a practical outcome. Or they cite the civilizing effect of great literature and the role played by history and philosophy in cultivating the human spirit.

These answers point toward matters that are both true and important, but they do little to address the question of why society should support professors to engage in recondite research on Wordsworth or Kant.

This question can be answered, for the societal challenges we face today are fundamentally humanistic in character, involving questions of history, beauty, personal identity, the sacred, the emplotting of scientific insights, and our response to the inevitable limits of knowledge and planning. Is nature, for instance, best understood as merely the raw material of our manufacturing processes? Are there reasons other than prudence for restraining our constantly expanding consumer lifestyle? And how do we balance the imperatives of expertise and democracy? The humanities have shown a laudable concern with such questions: the problems we face are profound, and nuanced reflection is absolutely necessary. But the humanities are guilty of not complementing these investigations with an account of their pertinence to our common lives. Philosophy is, by its very nature, an exercise in abstraction. This fact should be praised rather than apologized for; the skill of discerning the significant quality within a thousand details lies at the heart of thinking. But even as it embraces the most far-flung abstraction, philosophy must simultaneously retain a regard for the personal or social forces that animate it.

At least since Descartes's *Discourse* (1637), philosophy has prided itself on examining every presumption and prejudice; but both within and outside the academy we find an unquestioned consensus: philosophers spend their time teaching and writing in the university. Whether coming from the analytic or continental school of philosophy, philosophers perform the same set of tasks: introducing nonmajors to subjects such as ethics, and training majors in the traditional disciplinary domains such as logic, the philosophy of science, and political philosophy. Most of these philosophy majors will move on to other fields, often the law, but for those who go on to graduate school, their future is laid out before them: they will become the next generation's professors of philosophy.

In addition to teaching, contemporary philosophers engage in research that issues in the production of articles and books. With the exception of a few textbooks, philosophical writings consist of professional productions written for experts in the various philosophical subfields of specialization. As for writings meant to reach the populace, whether the general public or those in other parts of the knowledge industry, very few philosophers make the attempt. Books like

Alasdair MacIntyre's *After Virtue* are exceptions that prove the rule. Such works are viewed by academics, when they are considered at all, as a sign of a lack of philosophical seriousness.

The upshot of these efforts is a discipline that produces work of great intellectual quality and little relevance to the larger world. It does not seem to have occurred to many within either philosophy or society that philosophers could be doing something other than explaining books and writing scholarly articles within the academy. But is this the only—or best—way to do philosophy? Or can philosophers, *as philosophers*, participate in the political sphere, work in government or business, build a cabin, or go on a hike? That is, can we not merely apply the insights of philosophy to these activities, but engage in these activities *as* philosophy? Is philosophy necessarily tied to *logos* in the sense of words, as Aristotle claimed in understanding truth as a function of language, residing in the truth or falsity of statements about the world? Or might there be a form of *logos* and truth that is incarnate, an embodied philosophy through which one enacts philosophy within the community or the natural world? Could there be a philosophy—and by extension, a humanities—that, without becoming superficially pragmatic, takes on the juxtaposition of Aristotle and climate change, or semiotic theory and geologic fieldwork, in order to see what the effects are on both?

Geo-Logic treats philosophy (and by extension, the humanities) as a practice as well as a linguistic activity. "Practice" is here meant in the Buddhist sense—that wisdom cannot be wisdom if it only consists of a set of propositions. Wisdom must also be embodied, manifesting itself personally and socially in a daily performance. Indeed, until philosophy becomes a practice we can have little confidence in a philosopher's conclusions. Practicing philosophy means something more than applying the established insights of philosophy to our lives; we must approach philosophy as a yoga—a disciplined and embodied way of being in the world that in turn influences our philosophical propositions. The point is not to dismiss philosophy's discursive element, but to view the linguistic and the embodied, engaged aspects of philosophy as complementary. In this view of philosophy, philosophers would spend roughly equal amounts of time out in the "field" and in teaching and writing. "The preamble of thought, the transition through which it passes from the unconscious to the conscious, is action."[10]

Consider the way that Buddhism and Hinduism treat these questions. For all their differences (e.g., on the nature of the self,

God, and the cosmos) Buddhist practice and Hindu yogic techniques share a vision largely missing from Western philosophy: both emphasize the unity of our physical and contemplative lives and the practical and embodied nature of wisdom. Buddhism eschews speculation for an insistence upon the lived aspects of wisdom. The Japanese tradition of Buddhism especially focuses on the relation to everyday life through a set of *do* or Ways. Skills such as archery, flower arrangement, tea making, and fencing are all treated as occasions for gaining insight. Zen koans are based upon the belief that reason is an inadequate vehicle for expressing truth: a koan can be solved only through inspiration or action. Possibly the most rigorous of the Ways is judo, which trains the entire body rather than focusing on a particular technique. But even household activities such as washing the dishes and sweeping the floor are occasions for insight. "If a Zen student is sufficiently alive, he can practice the Way in the simplest activities of daily life."[11]

Similarly, yoga is a five-thousand-year-old Indian philosophical-religious system designed to unite the body, mind, and spirit. Like the word "religion," "yoga" means to tie or bind together: yoga is Sanskrit for "yoke" or "union." Westerners think of yoga in terms of its physical aspect, hatha yoga, in which adepts practice a set of asanas or postures. Within the Hindu tradition, however, physical training and meditation are two aspects of one process. Traditional yoga emphasizes an eightfold system of spiritual development including ethical disciplines (yama and niyama, restraints and observances), postures, breathing exercises, control of the senses, concentration, meditation, and absorption.

To suggest that Western philosophy, and more generally the humanities, be treated as a yoga implies that the theoretical and the practical be yoked in both our personal and public lives. Rather than the scholar's study, the native home of philosophy lies in the crafts we master: violin, pottery, and dance; scientific fieldwork, salesmanship, and political deal making; and, yes, teaching, writing, and research. Mindful of the practice and care needed to develop such skills, craftspeople of different skills are able to recognize one another. Great skill in any craft requires that we subordinate our desires to the work before us. Dedicating oneself to a craft is the sine qua non of freedom. Such craft work is implicit philosophy. Through practicing and eventually mastering such crafts, we create an experiential complement to philosophy's linguistic aspect.

IV.

In addition to the projects of rethinking the nature and roles of geology and philosophy in society, a third point needs emphasis here: *Geo-Logic* is an essay in topical thinking.

Topical thinking begins from both natural and geographical locations—"places" in the literal sense of the word—and from personal and social circumstances, the metaphorical sense of "place" implicit when we ask someone, "Tell me where you're coming from." Imagine you are on a trip to Morocco. Turning a corner in Marrakech, you glimpse a picturesque gathering of Muslim women. You lift the camera to capture the scene, and the group explodes: heads duck, backs turn, and hands raise before faces. Topical thinking begins from places like this, launched from a personal anecdote or a telling example, and acknowledging the circumstances that motivate thinking. From such beginnings, topical thinking follows a nomadic path that traces the implicit logic of a problem wherever it leads: perhaps from politics to sociology, then to economics, ethics, aesthetics, and theology, and finally back again to politics. From the experience of picture taking in Morocco, for instance, one might be led to ask how cameras enframe and objectify others, or to investigate the politics of gender, or to interrogate the role of tourism in intercultural communication—or from one to another of these problems.

Topical thinking organizes knowledge differently from the approach that governs academia, where research is structured in terms of the logical space of disciplines (chemistry, history, and the like). Topical thinking does not, however, abandon the disciplinary structure that defines knowledge today. A disciplinary approach to knowledge is not unreasonable, but it is partial. It needs to be complemented by an approach that remembers that our problems are always extra-disciplinary in nature. A medical patient, for instance, consists of something more than a series of "disciplines" (or systems: cardiac, pulmonary, digestive, and so on) worked on by medical professionals. As necessary as an understanding of these different systems is for treating a patient, medical practice suffers when it loses sight of the fact that it is a transdisciplinary entity (namely, a *person*) that is being treated. Likewise, our environmental problems resist simple division into the categories of environmental science, economics, and ethics. To confront these problems effectively we must understand how these categories relate and flow into one another at a particular location. Topical thinking is a means for tracing the ontological disruptions that occur when we attend closely to a problem.

Granted, it makes sense to divide a complex issue into parts, simplifying a problem in order to get a better hold of it. But if we never aim for a sense of the whole, seeking to understand the relation between and across the disciplines, we will be left with systematic incoherence: experts misunderstanding one another, and none of these experts able to converse with the public. For example, the United States government has spent more than a decade, and over 4 billion dollars, in a site characterization of Yucca Mountain, Nevada, in order to certify it as a safe repository for seventy thousand tons of the nation's civilian nuclear waste. Congress has mandated that the site must be confirmed safe for the next ten thousand years. Visit Yucca Mountain (a hundred miles north of Las Vegas) and climb down into Trench 14, a place notorious for the controversies it has generated. Are the calcite deposits found in Trench 14 meteoric, the result of rainwater percolating down from the surface? Or are they signs of hydraulic pumping, by which ground water has been forced up from below? If the latter is true, then this location has been affected by wide fluctuations of the water table, raising the possibility that the canisters of nuclear waste could be flooded, causing the nuclear waste to explode.[12] As one talks with government hydrologists, the terms of the debate begin to shift: from the intricacies of data interpretation, to competing hydrological models and computer techniques (each implying radically different accounts of the repository's future), to the relation between the state of Nevada and the federal government, to scientists' ethical obligations to inform the public, to our own responsibilities to future generations. The disciplines simplify—and falsify—the challenge of Yucca Mountain by beginning with the presumption that these questions can be dealt with independently of one another.

Over the last two decades the philosopher Alphonso Lingis has been perhaps the foremost representative of a topical approach to thinking. In a series of works, Lingis has tested the bounds of abstract academic discourse, juxtaposing existential encounters with insights mined from the history of philosophy.[13] While Lingis's main concern has been the confrontation with foreign cultures rather than with the natural world, his work has emphasized—more through example than argument—that thinking must be seen as a response to, rather than the delimiter of, experience. Like Lingis's work, *Geo-Logic* comes to these questions from the perspective of nineteenth- and twentieth-century continental philosophy, in particular the existential and hermeneutic perspectives of Heidegger and Merleau-Ponty. Nonetheless, how I use these thinkers may be as foreign to continental philosophers as to those with an analytic background in philosophy.

Given this topical approach, it is reasonable to offer a short account of my own "place" that led to the present study. It was the philosophic attractions of geology that led to my resigning a faculty position in philosophy to return for a master's degree. The point was not to approach the Earth sciences as a subspecies of the philosophy of science. Rather, I hoped to develop a scientifically informed phenomenology of the Earth that united geologic knowledge with philosophic insight to help us understand how to live on Earth. I had already spent some time in the field with geologists, and had been struck by how their thinking was affected by walking the land and interpreting its signs. Despite their invariably positivistic descriptions of the reasoning process within geologic fieldwork, I found that geologists practiced a type of earthbound phenomenology rather than an activity best described by the covering laws of the philosophy of science.

My intentions, then, were focused on developing a phenomenology of geology. But I soon discovered that geology as a discipline and a social institution was in a state of flux. I also discovered that the motivations of my fellow graduate students were markedly different from what I had imagined. Few of them pursued their course work for financial reasons—a point obvious to anyone familiar with the job market in the Earth sciences. And while I found the geopoetic aspects of their science everywhere within their labors—imagining worlds outside the compass of anyone's experience—this topic led a decidedly subterranean existence. Not only were the perspectives of philosophy and the humanities unfamiliar to them, they were also highly suspect. For a field suffering its own identity crisis—cuts in funding and a fear that, in the words of the physicist Luis Alvarez, fields such as paleontology may be nothing more than a type of stamp collecting—the last thing geologists needed was someone to draw out the connections between geology and the humanities.[14] Better to emphasize the rigorous nature of the field, and geology's ties to geochemistry and geophysics.

I found, however, that our interests intersected when they were reframed in terms of epistemology and politics. Scientists are people who go to great lengths to make sense of things. This drive takes a distinctive form within the Earth sciences, where much of the evidence is lost, and what remains is bent, warped, baked, or dismem-

bered. To be a field geologist, one must positively delight in conun-
drums, much as Sherlock Holmes enjoyed the complexities of his
profession. What's more, Earth scientists commonly combine their
fascination with epistemological puzzles with serious ethical and political concerns. Typically individuals with a profound feeling for nature (although the forms of this feeling vary widely), they often
champion conservationist and/or preservationist stances toward the
natural world.

Under the influence of my new colleagues, I soon found myself
focusing upon the epistemological and institutional as well as the
phenomenological and philosophical aspects of the Earth sciences.
Indeed, a new thought came to the fore: we need to understand how
all the domains of the humanities—epistemology and ethics, aesthetics and politics, metaphysics and theology—manifest themselves
in the study of the Earth. My goal at the outset was to develop a geologically informed environmental ethics and a phenomenology of
the Earth. But by the time I finished my degree, the goal had become to provide an ontology of the Earth sciences: to describe how
the various domains of knowledge (science, ethics, politics, aesthetics, metaphysics, and theology) are revealed within the discipline,
and how these domains relate to one another in various environmental controversies.

This ontological reevaluation of geology is being driven by the
most pragmatic of conditions. Both natural and cultural forces are
changing the role of the Earth/environmental sciences in society,
forcing the discipline to take on political responsibilities markedly
different from those of its own earlier history, as well as from most
other sciences. Whatever might be a scientist's private motivations,
the overall role of science in culture has long been as an "enabler"—
increasing the range of our power and control through the development of science-based technological development. This explains the
massive federal support of science (in 2000, around 40 billion dollars
for funding of non-defense-related science), and reflects our society's
desire for an ever expanding power over nature.

In its early years, geology fit within this framework—if not entirely comfortably. As geology emerged as a separate discipline in the
early nineteenth-century, the field straddled two roles: its discovery
of the history of life profoundly affected how we understand our
place in the cosmos, while it also served as a handmaiden to industrial development, providing raw materials for the industrial machine.[15] Certainly both of these roles continue today—although the
former, metaphysical issue is too often reduced to stale debates over

scientific creationism. But I wish to emphasize a third role that is coming to the fore: the Earth sciences as herald of local and planetary thresholds. The Earth sciences are becoming the sciences of limit, adding a cautionary note to our plans and ambitions. It is a simple point, but one that has taken us a long time to acknowledge: the world is not infinite. It is foolhardy to assume that we can endlessly exchange cultural for natural capital, escaping from every problem of scarcity or pollution via the development of new scientific and technological insights. Moreover, this question of scarcity is itself a prime example of the transdisciplinary nature of the Earth/ environmental sciences. The scarcity we are facing will not be a matter of running up against purely physical boundaries. Scarcity in the twenty-first century will combine physical limits with a complex range of cultural factors such as economics, politics (i.e., questions of justice), aesthetics (quality-of-life issues), and theology (a sense of the sacred). In this third role, the Earth sciences will function as an early warning system for geo-ecological calamities—as the eyes and ears of the body politic. This new role will put especially strong pressure upon the Earth sciences to become a bridge discipline spanning the sciences and the humanities.

V.

To chart this ontological disruption, *Geo-Logic* begins from three places or topoi: (1) the political controversies surrounding acid mine drainage (chapters 2 and 3); (2) the nature of scientific research as it is conducted in the field (chapters 4, 5, and 6); and (3) the challenges facing public Earth scientists as they seek to serve the needs of communities (chapters 7 and 8). In each of these locations I explore how reconfiguring the disciplines of the Earth sciences and philosophy casts new light on our environmental challenges. My claim is straightforward: we are not making good use of our intellectual resources, in large part because of the disciplinary presumptions that dominate the production of knowledge today. Addressing societal problems will require a type of transdisciplinarity that moves both horizontally (across the disciplines) and vertically (between intellectual culture and society at large). To gain a purchase on our environmental problems requires that we break down the divide separating the natural and cultural aspects of geology, *and* that we make philosophy into a cultural practice as well as a linguistic event. Rewriting the disciplines of the Earth/environmental sciences and philosophy will provide communities with new resources for creating an environmentally sustainable future.

Geo-Logic starts with a hike in the San Juan Mountains of southwest Colorado. Reconceiving the Earth sciences and philosophy begins at ten thousand feet, with the problem of acid mine drainage. Hard rock mining's legacy is deeply ambiguous, leaving us with, on the one hand, picturesque mine works, and, on the other, dead streams and a scarred landscape. The controversy over acid mine drainage is labyrinthine. It leads us to questions that are at turns scientific, political, metaphysical, aesthetic, and even theological in nature. But we shall find our way out of our environmental problems only by exploring each of these passages in all their multi-disciplinary variety.

The argument then turns to an investigation of geology's distinctive epistemological status. Epistemology—i.e., the theory of knowledge—seems an arcane subject; but our sense of what counts as real knowledge circumscribes our social and political conversations. The absence of anything like a philosophy of *field* science is telling, for field-based sciences such as geology offer a better account than do the laboratory sciences of both the power and limits of science for addressing societal problems. Scientific reasoning is still too often seen as a mechanical process that provides us with authoritative, even infallible answers—a misrepresentation that damages both science and society. Indeed, with the rise of computer simulations, the positivist spirit, once thought slain, is again in ascendance. In contrast, the reasoning process typified by scientific fieldwork offers an account of reasoning that is more applicable to life's uncertainties. Seldom possessing all the knowledge we would like, we fill in the gaps in our knowledge with interpretation and reasonable assumptions that we hope will someday be confirmed. Field-based sciences exemplify this process, mirroring the complexities we face in our personal and political lives.

Third, *Geo-Logic* moves into the halls and offices of public Earth-science agencies in search of a political philosophy of science. The philosophy of science and political theory have long been considered disjunct domains. Public science agencies challenge this divorce, for they exist to serve the common good, to further societal values such as freedom, justice, and community. Agencies such as the U.S. Geological Survey (USGS), the National Aeronautics and Space Administration (NASA), and the Geological Survey of Canada (GSC) inhabit a space that is at once scientific and political. Yet there is, to date, no political philosophy of public science.

The USGS and the GSC are organizations in transition: much of their traditional work (e.g., geologic and topographic mapping) is ending, and critics ask why private industry cannot take over the functions that remain.[16] This question itself reveals the gap in our culture's thinking about the nature of the public realm, for public science agencies have a critical role to play in an era of environmental limits. Nevertheless, realizing this opportunity will require that agencies such as the USGS and the GSC embrace a wider definition of scientific responsibility—one that charges them with the task of understanding and responding to community values in addition to their traditional commitment to scientific excellence. Exploring the public or political responsibilities of these institutions provides us with a powerful example of how we can create new conceptual and political spaces, freeing both science and society from epistemological prejudices that have stymied our culture's conversation.

We begin by turning to a place where the full range of our geological concerns is manifest: the controversies surrounding acid mine drainage.

2

ACID MINE PHILOSOPHY

I.

The San Juans are possibly the most beautiful mountains in Colorado. To see for yourself, take the trail up to Ice Lakes Basin. Blue spruce and quaking aspen cover the flanks of the mountains that rise to snow-topped peaks. Naturally occurring mineral oxides paint the rocky slopes above tree line yellow and red, while the trees themselves sprout from pale limestones, ruddy sandstones, ancient lava flows, and beds of welded volcanic ash. Ridge lines stand jagged against the sky: rather than eroding like granite, which peels like the layers of an onion, the sedimentary rocks of the San Juans break along or across bedding planes, all edges and sharp angles. Ancient glaciers have also left their mark: eighteen thousand years ago, the streams of ice reached deep down the valleys of the San Juans, carving grand, U-shaped troughs along the Animas, the San Juan, and the San Miguel Rivers. Still relatively unvisited, these mountains today contain three wilderness areas. If they were an hour from Denver the San Juans would be a national park.

It's all the more striking, then, when the trail turns and you find an awful mess. Dilapidated mine works, rotten timbers askew, block part of a gaping black portal. Jumbled masses of waste rock dumped from the mine entrance have slid down the mountainside to Ice Lakes Creek. Abandoned motors, twisted pipes, and corrugated sheet metal rust in the sun. Thick rivulets of orange gunk leak from the mine and run downhill to the creek, contaminating rainwater and snowmelt with sulfuric acid and a variety of heavy metals—zinc, copper, cadmium, lead, iron, aluminum. In many of the streams of the San Juans, low pH and toxic metals have killed all the fish, both directly by their toxicity and indirectly by destroying the habitats of insects that they feed upon (GL:CH2).

19

The problem is called acid mine drainage—shorthand for concerns with abandoned mine lands and the streams that run across them. Like many of our environmental problems, acid mine drainage has sparked intense debate. In towns like Silverton, Colorado, the controversy is over whether these areas should be restored. But to what standard, and at whose cost? The debate rages in national and global venues, but perhaps most fiercely in the American West, where acid mine drainage is the single greatest water quality problem. It is a debate with a wide range of interested parties. Stakeholders in this dispute include landowners and local officials, environmental organizations and mining companies, federal agencies and lawyers, scientists, tourists, and local businessmen.

There is, of course, a standard way to settle such disputes—through the artful combination of science and public policy. Science provides the facts needed for decision-making, and the law represents the will of the people: Lee's compass and gyroscope. But to adequately address our environmental problems we need more than good science and democratic policy. We also need philosophy.

For many, the word "philosophy" summons up an image of Rodin's Thinker: a naked man, fist to chin, turning in upon himself in rapt reflection. Or perhaps of Socrates in a toga, distracting people from their daily tasks by asking a series of pointless questions. But philosophy worthy of its name (*philos-sophia*, the love of wisdom) begins on the ground, scrambling over scree, poking around in just such unsightly holes as the abandoned mines in the San Juans. In its best dress, philosophy wears hiking boots and carries a walking stick. It wanders nature trails that lead into the heart of our cultural wildernesses and the deeper, psychic sources of our environmental problems.

Philosophy can play two critical roles in environmental controversies like acid mine drainage. First, it can provide an account of the specifically philosophic aspects of our environmental problems, the ethical, aesthetic, epistemological, metaphysical, and theological dimensions that we must acknowledge before we can solve. These dimensions are more central to our concerns with the environment than we often acknowledge: in many cases, the law and scientific data are stalking horses disguising the fundamentally philosophic nature of our concerns.

Second, philosophy can offer a synopsis of how the various disciplines relate within a given problem. Questions such as acid mine drainage refuse to follow strict disciplinary boundaries. They require a logic that is willing to track an argument across all the domains of knowledge: hydrology, chemistry, public policy, politics, aesthetics, metaphysics, and theology. Neither is the relationship between these different domains static: when we consider a problem, there is an inner movement to the topic that drives our thinking from one discipline to the next. Hegel called this movement *dialectic:* thinking advances through our recognition of the inadequacy of the current formulation of a problem. For Hegel, these contradictions within our thinking drive us toward a wider, richer, more synthetic understanding of the problem. This movement of thought is at the same time a movement in the world, for the challenges we face—environmental or otherwise—overflow every category. Since the *logos* of the world is dynamic and embodied, our thinking must follow the internal logic of the issue at hand.[1]

It is, of course, impossible to give a complete account of a problem such as acid mine drainage. Indeed, it will become clear that we are unable to give a *complete* account of *any part* of controversies such as this one—although the continued narrowing of academic disciplines suggests that dreams of mastery through expertise live on. Rather than a complete account, the goal here is to provide a fractured narrative of the acid mine drainage controversy. Like a cubist painting (e.g., Georges Braque's *Candlestick and Playing Cards on a Table,* GL:CH2), our goal should be to show the same object simultaneously from several points of view. But to a greater degree than in some cubist works, one hopes a recognizable picture emerges, made up of sets of angles, none of which dominates all the others.

By addressing these two needs, philosophy can bring to our environmental problems what we sorely lack: a sense of the whole. How do scientific truths relate to our lived experience of the world? Or the facts of economics with the less tangible but no less real concerns with community values and quality of life? By investigating the conceptual background of other disciplines the philosopher can gain high ground to survey them all. The philosopher may not possess the scientific background to judge the robustness of a specific hydrological model, or the economic expertise needed to compute the per diem cost of running an abandoned mine's water treatment plant. But he or she should have the conceptual agility to help people understand the limits of mathematical models for understanding the real world, and to contrast the cost of the treatment plant against the community's political, recreational, aesthetic, and metaphysical interests.

It is precisely this role that has been missing from our environmental debates. In an information-rich age such as ours, when we can find massive, seemingly infinite amounts of knowledge on al-most any subject, what we lack—precisely *through* of this glut of in-formation—is a grasp of the whole. This sense of the whole was what "logic" originally meant. For the Greeks, *logos* did not simply mean the mechanical deduction of conclusions from premises, or the linking of cause and effect. Rather, *logos* connoted the sense of ori-entation and placement that comes from knowing how things hang together. Our society, then, while having made a monumental effort in scientific and technical reasoning, has in this sense become deeply illogical.

II.

The veins may have played out, and the mines lie quiet—at least until the next jump in the metals market. But the legacy of mining remains. A casual car-tour of the San Juans is enough to alert one to controversy. The San Juans contain more than fifteen hundred abandoned mines. Depending on one's opinions about aes-thetics, history, and nature, these old mines, buildings, mine dumps, and tailing ponds are either picturesque, an eyesore, or a sacrilege. What cannot be denied is that many of the streams of the upper An-imas run orange, their water, rocks, and banks stained red and cov-ered with a thick sludge. The lack of aquatic life in many stretches has raised concerns about how healthy it is to drink the water or eat the fish that remain—concerns for the people of Silverton, for those downriver in Durango, Colorado, and Farmington, New Mexico, and for the tourists who visit the area.

While not a household term, acid mine drainage is a problem of wide effect. It is a serious issue in the eastern United States, where the source is usually coal rather than gold mining. Acid mine drainage has also caused substantial problems around the world, in places such as Spain, Eastern Europe, Peru, and Indonesia.[2] The American West is home to several hundred thousand abandoned mines that have contaminated thousands of miles of streams. Sites and streams needing attention may number in the thousands. The Mineral Policy Center estimates that the cleanup in the United States will total between 32 and 72 billion dollars.[3]

In the San Juans, questions concerning acid mine drainage cen-ter upon the upper Animas drainage in the high mountains and val-leys surrounding the town of Silverton. The confluence of three streams—Mineral Creek, Cement Creek, and the upper Animas—

define the drainage (figure 2.1). The Animas is not commercially navigable, unless you count rubber rafts and kayaks.[4] In its upper reaches it offers only a little fishing. It is mainly a source of beauty. The region is too high for crops, so there is no demand for irrigation; and while water quality remains a concern, Silverton has traditionally drawn its water supply from the Bear Creek drainage, an area that has never been mined.

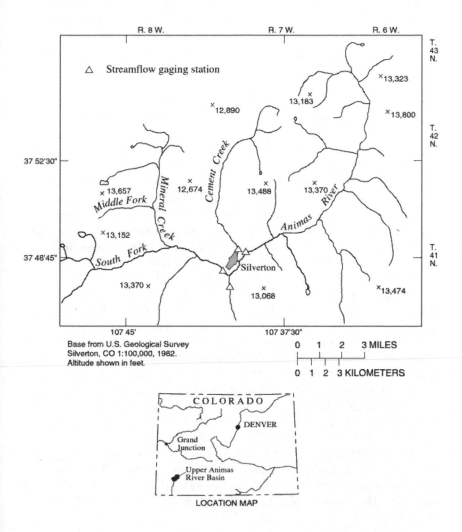

Base from U.S. Geological Survey
Silverton, CO 1:100,000, 1982.
Altitude shown in feet.

LOCATION MAP

The miners came for the gold and silver, but the mountains also contained large amounts of base metals (e.g., iron, lead) locked up with sulfur as sulfide compounds. Exposing the metal-bearing rock to air and water "mobilizes" these metals, releasing them as well as sulfuric acid into the streams. The pH of the upper Animas is in many cases low enough to cause aquatic life to be deformed or die. A low pH also allows the heavy metals to stay in solution, causing the high concentrations of metals in the water—killing more aquatic life. The metals themselves have a wide variety of effects upon the streams. Zinc, copper, and cadmium pass into the water column and kill fish through their toxicity. Aluminum and iron settle on the stream bottom and disrupt the physical habitat of bottom-dwelling creatures (such as stone flies and caddis flies) that the fish depend upon, by filling in the spaces in the streambed where the creatures breed.

Despite (and in some cases, because of) all this, the San Juans are a magnet for hikers, backpackers, horseback-riders, four-wheel enthusiasts, and history buffs. The area's historical attractions include a narrow-gauge railroad, ghost towns, and the old mines from the gold strike days. The centrally located town—village, really—of Silverton is ground zero for debates over the abandoned mine lands of the San Juans. Silverton rests at 9,300 feet in a deep valley where the sun sets early most of the year. In the winter, its population numbers around three hundred. Most of the shops are boarded up, with only the Avalanche Coffee Shop and the Miner's Tavern regularly open. In the winter months avalanches sometimes close U.S. 550, the only paved road into town; in 1993, Silverton had no mail service for a week. Many of the winter inhabitants are ex-miners and people who still identify quite strongly with the mining ethos: a popular bumper sticker in town reads: "Earth First. We'll mine the other planets later." Silverton's population expands in the summer with the arrival of absentee landowners and the owners of small shops and galleries. For a few months the town's character lies somewhere between mining town and tourist trap, living off of the stream of tourists deposited daily by the Durango and Silverton Narrow Gauge Railroad. Today the entire town is a National Historic Landmark, the local economy surviving on its history and the area's natural beauty (GL:CH2).

Silverton's mining past remains a palpable presence. Beginning in 1871, over 9 million ounces of gold have been taken from the mountains surrounding Silverton, the second-largest amount of any region in the state (the Cripple Creek district ranks first). Abandoned mine works are everywhere, a reminder of the glory days when the town was something more than a tourist destination. Since the mid-1870s, Silverton has gone through a series of booms and busts. The town is still recovering from the most recent downturn, caused by the closing of the area's last major mine—the Sunnyside—in 1991. Mining has always been an episodic business. Someone makes a strike, setting off a free-for-all. Then consolidation sets in as the business is taken over by large interests. Sooner or later the ore plays out, and the companies and the miners move on. Repeated hundreds of times throughout the West, this cycle has left a legacy of old mine works and water problems. If this cycle has now gone the way of other relics—itself a doubtful proposition—it is because mining corporations today have largely moved offshore to countries where the costs of land and labor and environmental regulations are significantly less than those in the United States.

The closing of the Sunnyside mine is emblematic of changes across the entire U.S. mining industry. Like agriculture and logging, mining has become the domain of great corporations operating on economies of scale; medium-sized operations like the Sunnyside, unable to compete, have fallen to the wayside. Tunnel mining has also given way to open pit techniques like cyanide heap leach mining, first developed in New Zealand around 1900. Cyanide heap leaching has made it possible to cheaply mine extraordinarily minute quantities of precious metals—at the cost of grinding up entire mountains.

In cyanide heap leach mining, crushed rock is dumped on a plastic liner. Nozzles then spray a cyanide solution over the ore that pulls the gold from the rock. The gold-cyanide solution drains to the bottom of the pad, where a series of drains and pipes collect it. The gold is separated from the cyanide; the cyanide is then recycled. Approximately 90 percent of the world's gold currently comes from mines that use cyanide as their reagent (GL:CH2).

While cyanide (CN—a combination of carbon and nitrogen) breaks down quickly under sunlight, cyanide heap leaching is not entirely benign. The historic Summitville mine in Colorado's eastern San Juans—forty miles from the Animas drainage—was reopened in 1986 as a cyanide heap leach operation. Five years later, Galactic Resources, the company that ran the operation, declared bankruptcy and abandoned the site when it was discovered that the plastic pad was leaking cyanide. Summitville became an EPA Superfund site: as of 2001, U.S. taxpayers have spent 150 million dollars in attempts to remediate the area.[5]

III.

We began with a hiker's experience of abandoned mines and acid drainage. But the area's mining history can inspire as well as repel:

> But time has passed, the sounds have faded. The men are gone. Empty buildings stand against the weather. An unsecured door bangs mindlessly against the wooden side of a building once full of working machines run by men earnestly pursuing their dreams. Now, the countryside is quiet. Arrastra Creek, its gentle flow broken by mining debris, no longer tells its tales to passing miners. To be sure, an occasional lessee may come into the gulch and for a while a mine will run. But the boom is gone—the glory years are over.[6]

Seeing the conditions of the upper Animas as a *problem*, rather than as picturesque, requires a certain perspective, one not shared by all parties, and especially not by many of the locals. By what criterion does acid mine drainage count as a problem? What should count as a solution? Who decides who is responsible, and who should bear the costs of correcting these problems?

In the thousands of pages of material on acid mine drainage, one finds very little sustained reflection on these questions. Somehow we have slipped from fundamental (if devilishly difficult) questions to issues that are more easily answered. Like the man looking for his keys beneath the streetlamp because that's where he can see, our culture turns to science to deliver us from conflicting perspectives.

Make no mistake: a great deal of worthy scientific research on acid mine drainage has been and is being done. Science has identified the sources of pH and heavy metal contamination, the toxicity of pH and heavy metals in different species of fish and at different stages in their life cycle, and the natural background conditions of these streams before mining began. But few have considered the question: to what degree is acid mine drainage a scientific issue rather than an economic, ethical, aesthetic, or theological one? Certainly, part of the reason for this is that we know how to conduct scientific research and economic analyses—not to minimize the difficulty of such work—while our culture has largely given up on thinking through the ethical, aesthetic, and theological aspects of societal controversies like acid mine drainage. It has been drummed into our heads that these latter topics are not susceptible to rational treatment.

In fact, it is not possible to point to any one particular law, one set of facts, one individual, or one group as having triggered the last ten years of controversy in the San Juans. Like the river itself, events flow together, combining in unpredictable ways. Issues of law and public policy play off of individual personalities, tradition and precedent pair off against scientific data, and supposedly objective scientific data are found to include value judgments and assumptions. Surrounding all this are the economic realities and primordial human responses to a landscape that embodies the history and ideals of the people who live within and care for these mountains. Every account frames the story differently, emphasizing one perspective while casting the others into shadow.

In the minds of many, it was the Federal Clean Water Act (CWA) that drove the acid mine controversy in the San Juans. The CWA does provide a useful framework for this debate, determining much of what happens on the level of policy. Even here, however, matters become sticky. Some of the locals claim that the Clean Water Act only became applicable after a local county commissioner and others backpacked fish into parts of the upper Animas drainage able to support fish. (Certain parts of the Clean Water Act are operative only if a stream contains fish.) It is notable that no national and local environmental organizations demanded an investigation into acid mine drainage. Neither did the citizens of Durango and Silverton, the two towns most likely to be affected by water problems, raise the alarm. In fact, local participation, in the form of the Animas River Stakeholders Group, was first organized by an outside organization, the State of Colorado. By their own account, local citizens and officials at first rejected attempts at organization. They overcame their reluctance only out of the fear that if they did not, state and federal agencies would dictate solutions from afar.

In 1972, Congress enacted the Federal Water Pollution Control Act. The Clean Water Act supplemented this statute in 1977. Both acts, with subsequent amendments in 1981, 1987, and 1993, are known as the "Clean Water Act" or CWA.[7] The Clean Water Act seeks to protect the nation's navigable waters by setting water quality standards for surface waters.[8] It also regulates discharges into these waters throughout the United States. The Clean Water Act calls for the "restoring and maintaining of the chemical, physical, and biological integrity of the nation's waters."[9] (The debate thus turns in part on how to interpret the humanistic term "integrity" in a given situation.) To achieve this, it requires states to establish water quality standards for every river basin in the United States.

The CWA also establishes a permit system to regulate point-source discharges (a point-source of pollution is a discrete, identifiable source of discharge: a pipe or a ditch, for instance; non-point sources lack a single identifiable location, for instance, agricultural and street runoff). Polluters are issued NPDES (National Pollutant Discharge Elimination System) permits that describe the stream-specific water quality standards that their effluents must meet.

The Environmental Protection Agency has the final jurisdiction to enforce the Clean Water Act. However, as a matter of policy, the EPA grants states or tribal authorities primacy over the application and enforcement of the Clean Water Act to meet its federal standards. The EPA still retains overall responsibility under the act. It approves all state rules and regulations, and oversees state enforcement. The EPA may also take independent action when it believes that a state's programs do not adequately meet federal standards. This presents a potential dilemma for companies and municipalities. Even if they satisfy state requirements, the EPA may still step in and raise the bar. More commonly, however, the EPA arm-twists by threatening to take over a program until the state issues the rules and regulations that the EPA wants.[10]

The 1972 Act called for the nation to establish interim water quality goals by 1983. In response, the State of Colorado began moving toward controlling the Animas drainage in 1979, when the Colorado Water Quality Control Commission (the WQCC) established use classifications and water standards for the Animas. At that time, the WQCC did not even try to classify the upper reaches of the Animas, because so much of it was devoid of fish and macro-invertebrates. As noted, this changed in 1985, when locals started stocking the local streams and lakes. Whether these streams contained fish prior to mining is a historical question difficult to answer.

In 1991 the Colorado Water Quality Control Division (a different group from the WQCC; part of the Colorado Department of Public Health and Environment, the CDPHE) started collecting water quality data in the upper Animas, a program it continued through 1993. According to the Colorado Center for Environmental Management (CCEM), a nonprofit organization formed by Colorado's governor Roy Romer to identify solutions to environmental management problems, "this monitoring was prompted by a long-term need to better understand mine-related problems in the area and impacts across the Basin."[11] One might surmise that the hammer of the Clean Water Act also played a role in the decision to monitor the streams.

In 1991, however, the slow grind of the bureaucratic machinery surrounding the Clean Water Act began to intersect with a second set of events. In that year the Sunnyside Gold Mine ceased operations. Echo Bay Mines, Inc., had bought the Sunnyside Mine in 1986, but after five years of losses Echo Bay closed the operation. Gold production had never reached the expected levels, and with the continued low price of gold, the company decided to cut its losses.[12] Sunnyside Gold Corporation (now a subsidiary of Echo Bay) had a reclamation plan for the mine, which called for the removal of mining buildings, the consolidation and revegetation of waste rock and mine tailings, and the diversion of surface water flowing from the mine. But final closure required that Sunnyside submit its reclamation plan to the Colorado Division of Minerals and Geology.

The Colorado Division of Minerals and Geology approved the overall reclamation plan. But Sunnyside also needed the Department of Public Health and Environment to release them from their NPDES permit for the water that was leaving the site. The flow from the mine, which averaged two thousand gallons per minute, was only mildly acidic, but it did contain high levels of zinc and iron. Prior to the Clean Water Act, the water had flowed directly into Cement Creek. In the 1970s, however, the previous mining operator had built a water treatment plant that operated under a NPDES water discharge permit that had been issued by the CDPHE. By the early 1990s, Sunnyside Gold was spending $500,000 dollars a year to run this plant, which cleaned the mine water before it flowed into Cement Creek and eventually the Animas.[13]

As part of its mine closure plan, Sunnyside proposed to plug the mine entrance (known as the American Tunnel) and discontinue treating the water coming from the mine. Sunnyside claimed that the mine works would quickly fill with water, and the water within the tunnels and adits would reach a chemical equilibrium similar to natural background conditions. The output from the mine portal would stop, and any new springs that appeared across the mountain would have the pH and metal loading natural to the region. Sunnyside would achieve its goal—financial closure to its involvement at the site—with no negative effects upon the Animas drainage.

But matters did not end here. The CDPHE objected to Sunnyside's plan on two grounds. First, the treated water entering Cement Creek from the mine actually *improved* the water quality of the creek, which had been affected by both natural and anthropogenic (human-caused) sources upstream of the mine. To plug the portal would therefore have the net effect of degrading the water quality of Cement Creek. Second, the CDPHE had doubts about Sunnyside's plans for controlling the waters within the mine. The natural conditions of the mountain had been irretrievably changed: over the years, continued dynamiting had fractured and hollowed out whole sections of the mountain. Furthermore, the production of acid drainage is greatly accelerated by exposing rocks to a mixture of water and air. Driving hundreds of adits and tunnels into the mountain had created the perfect combination of air and water to produce acid drainage. Sunnyside Gold's plan was to keep the site entirely wet, thus turning off the production of excess acid drainage. The CDPHE, however, was far from sure that the flooded mine would equilibrate to natural background, doubts based upon complex geochemical and structural considerations.[14] It therefore refused to let Sunnyside out from under its water discharge permit obligations, claiming that any new seeps that developed in the surrounding mountains after they plugged the American Tunnel would be subject to NPDES regulations. Sunnyside's response was to sue in state court.

In May 1996, Sunnyside and the State of Colorado reached an out-of-court settlement. As part of this agreement, Sunnyside signed a Consent Decree that stated that it would clean up an "A" list of abandoned mined sites in the San Juans. The hope was that in doing so, Sunnyside would remove zinc and iron discharges roughly equal to the amounts coming from the American Tunnel prior to treatment. Sunnyside would continue to monitor zinc levels at a site known as A72 (on the Animas just downriver of Silverton) for five years after the cleanup was completed. If zinc loading remained at or below an agreed-upon baseline level (approximately 550 parts per million, ppm) over this period, the state would release Sunnyside from its permit. Sunnyside could shut down its water treatment plant and walk away, or turn the treatment plant over to someone else. If for some reason conditions did not improve, Sunnyside had a "B" list of abandoned sites in the San Juans that could be remediated.

By 1999, the remediation work on all of the orphaned sites on the "A" list had been completed. To date, monitoring at A72 has not shown any improvement in zinc levels, despite the fact that Sunnyside continues to run its water treatment plant. These circumstances have understandably left officials at Sunnyside Gold searching for explanations.[15]

We will return later to the issues raised by this Consent Decree. First, however, note how the terms of this debate have shifted. Acid mine drainage became a problem through legal defin-ition: the Clean Water Act drove the debate in the San Juans. But the terms of Sunnyside's mine closure now turned, not only on the details and the interpretation of the Clean Water Act, but also upon our understanding of the chemistry, hydrology, and geology of the region. What would happen if the American Tunnel was plugged? Why are there no effects from the cleanup of the "A" sites? We find ourselves at a site of ontological disruption, as the boundaries between our disciplinary categories begin to slip and give way. The debate has moved from the interpretation of admin-istrative law to the interpretation of geologic facts and hydrological models. Let us, then, leave the Clean Water Act and focus our at-tention on the situation on the ground—and beneath it.

IV.

Approaching the San Juan Mountains from the south, driving up the Animas River valley past the towns of Durango and Hermosa, one passes massive cliffs of red and buff-colored sedimentary strata that dip to the south. Coming to the San Juans from the north past the towns of Ridgway and Ouray one faces a similar scene, but now the layers dip to the north. It is as if a titanic force had pushed the sedimentary beds from below, tilting the beds until it burst through at what is now the center of the San Juans (GL:CH2).

This is roughly the account that geologists offer of the San Juan Mountains. The sloping sedimentary strata all point upward toward the center of the mountains, where one finds abundant evidence of volcanic activity: lava beds, welded ash flows, mineralized rocks, and deeply offset faults. In the mid-Tertiary, some 35 million years ago, southwest Colorado became a volcanic landscape. The source of the lava and ash was a huge mass of magma, which was also the source of the minerals that someday would interest the miners. The vol-canics continued for 10 million years; from the volume of the de-posits it seems that many of the explosions dwarfed those of Mount St. Helen and Mt. Pinatubo.

Silverton itself lies in the midst of the San Juan volcanic field, at the edge of an area that geologists call the Silverton caldera. A caldera is a volcano that has collapsed upon itself. After the explo-sive venting of its lava and ash the volcano gives way, leaving a con-cave depression. While the interpretation of the region is not child's play, the signs suggest periodic volcanic eruptions, leaving multiple, overlapping calderas in the region. (One estimate puts the number at fifteen.) A series of faults runs along the caldera's edge, and another set radiates from the volcano's center like the spokes of a wheel. These fractures served as the plumbing system for the upward flow of mineral fluids that precipitated in veins.

Seeing the caldera requires a practiced eye. The volcanic lavas and welded tuffs (the latter formed from superheated volcanic ash that falls like snow and welds together) are clear enough. So are the signs of mineralization: Red Mountain, north of Silverton, gets its name from the oxidized orange and red stains that cover its sides. But the geography has been transformed over the last 25 million years. Like a biblical parable, what was once high is now low, and vice versa: the land has become inverted. The faulted outside edge of the caldera allowed not only the passage of hydrothermal fluids from below, but also snowmelt and rainwater filtering down from above. Erosion attacked the ring faults, especially during the last 2 million years of glacial conditions. Thousands of feet of rock were removed, and the fault zones came to mark the paths of the river courses. Valleys were cut along the edge of the caldera as the area was elevated through uplift. Today the river courses of Mineral Creek and the Animas River define the south and west sides of the caldera rim (see fig. 2.1).

Two points may be drawn from this account. First, this description of astonishing events, evoking a landscape shaped by both fire and ice, functions simultaneously as a set of scientific, poetic, and theological statements. Rather than being immune from a sense of awe, the science of geology prompts and promotes our wonder. Second, note that long before the appearance of humans the region was a naturally mineralized area subject to acid drainage and heavy metal contamination. After all, it was these naturally occurring conditions that drew the miners to the region in the first place. Acid *mine* drainage is but an accelerated form of the natural processes of the acid *rock* drainage native to the area. Acid rock drainage results from natural weathering processes, biologic activity, and the regional geology. The problem, then, becomes how to clearly distinguish between acid mine and acid rock drainage. And it turns out that separating natural background conditions from human-caused acid drainage is a difficult and contentious matter.

The production of acid drainage is a complex process involving chemistry and biology as well as geology. Exposure of the sulfur-rich rocks to air and water causes the sulfide minerals (e.g., pyrite, galena, and sphalerite, made up of sulfer and iron, lead, and zinc respectively) to oxidize. Take the example of pyrite (FeS_2), also known as fool's gold. Rainwater, snowmelt, and exposure to air break the iron sulfate compound into its constituent parts, ferrous iron and sulfur, at a relatively slow rate. The sulfate ions react with the water to produce sulfuric acid, and the iron goes into the water as well. By itself, however, this chemical reaction is not energetic enough to produce very much acid drainage. But the reaction explodes with the presence of sulfur-oxidizing bacteria such as those of the genus *Thiobacilli*. *Thiobacilli* are chemolithotropes: they eat rocks. And *Thiobacilli* are ubiquitous in nature. They massively increase the chemical process, resulting in an immense expansion in the amount of acid drainage being produced.

The pH of a solution is a measure of its acidity, based upon a logarithmic scale; going down the scale, each number represents a tenfold increase in the amount of acidity. Thus the difference between a pH of 7 and one of 3 is four orders of magnitude, giving you a solution that is ten thousand times more acidic. The pH in streams of the upper Animas drops as low as 2 and 3 (lower than the pH of vinegar, and about the same as that of a car battery; trout die at pH values below 5.4). A low pH also allows the heavy metals to stay in solution, causing the high concentrations of metals in the water that lead to the fish kills. If the pH is buffered (that is, raised, say by passing over limestone), the metals will come out of solution, leaving bright orange-red stains coating the rocks on the sides and at the bottom of the stream. As noted above, this also destroys the habitats for the bugs that the fish depend upon.

One of the basic goals of the scientific study of acid mine drainage is to clearly distinguish between natural and anthropogenic acid drainage. The idea is that if we can tell the difference between the two, we will have solid criteria for what should be cleaned up. But distinguishing between natural and anthropogenic acid drainage is tricky. Of course, an old mine works, with its timbers askew and a thick rivulet of red gunk issuing from its portal, is a poster child for acid mine runoff (GL:CH2). But it remains an open question how much of that discharge has been generated through mining, and how much is simply the concentrated runoff that had previously found its way to the surface through unknown natural springs across the mountain. The geologist offers an educated guess; in this case, the majority of the drainage would probably be human-caused. But such open conditions give rise to differing interpretations and extended debates.

U.S. Geological Survey hydrologists have wrestled with the question of distinguishing between natural and anthropogenic acid drainage throughout the region. One part of the Animas drainage, the Middle Fork of Mineral Creek, was found to contain seventy-three springs and seventeen mines.[16] Of the mine sites, seven had water coming from their portals. Throughout the basin, hydrologists face the challenge of determining whether seemingly natural seeps are truly natural, or are rather the surface expression of mining-caused drainage further upslope. Sometimes the evidence is conclusive, but often hydrologists must try to map the faults and the mines in an area to guess at the possible relation between an old mine site and an apparently natural spring.

The fundamentally interpretive nature of fieldwork is typified by a spot known as Red Chemotroph Spring, in the Cement Creek drainage (GL:CH2). My class and I visited the site in June 1997, with Win Wright, a USGS hydrologist who in later publications offered this as a classic example of a natural mineral-rich seep. As we listened to his account of Red Chemotroph as a natural spring, I wandered upslope, and found two one-inch cables snaking down the mountain. Win thought the cables were the remnants of an old mine tramway that ran from Lark Mine to Cement Creek. Yes, there had been mining in the area, upslope from Red Chemotroph, but Win believed that it had had no influence upon either the existence or the development of the spring.

There was no reason to doubt his judgment; Win had spent years studying the region, hiking across nearly all the drainages, and he had a reputation among the locals for being fair-minded. And there was nothing unusual about such a judgment. The life of the scientist—especially the field scientist—is filled with situations such as this, judgment calls made on the basis of one's education, partial data, and years in the field. But instances such as these reveal the naïveté of treating science as the objective, ultimate arbiter of our environmental controversies.

Most of the science surrounding acid mine drainage involves similar acts of professional judgment. For instance, a stream's pH and mineral content can vary with both the time of day and the season. On a warm summer day, a small rivulet will be flushed with snowmelt by noon, a fact that will itself vary according to the previous winter's amount of snow. Readings in early June will differ from those in July or September as the snowpack declines. Readings by two people on the same day, at the same time, in two adjacent valleys, can still vary because of surface geology, recent sheep grazing, and weather conditions. Even the instruments measuring pH and conductivity can be thrown off by the lack of ions present in the

snowmelt. Measuring pH—the amount of protons in a solution—
requires a degree of background conductivity. But rain and snow are
often low in anions and cations. Unless the field worker adds potas-
sium chloride to the sample, the result will be off.

Adjusting for constantly changing conditions requires a nuanced sense of one's work, what the biologist Michael Polanyi calls
"personal knowledge."[17] In our culture this phrase is an oxymoron: if
a claim is personal, it cannot be real knowledge, and vice versa. On
this account, real knowledge must be objective, untainted by personal factors. But this puts scientists in the position of not being
able to acknowledge a major source of their understanding, the intuitive grasp that comes from years of working intimately with a
subject. We always make more of our experiences than can ever be
tallied; walking the outcrop or working in the lab, we quietly absorb
a thousand small signs that lie beneath every lawlike generalization. Scientific reasoning, like reasoning in general, depends on
deliberation and judgment. Such judgment depends upon the ability—and the opportunity, increasingly rare in a Pentium-driven culture—to deliberate. Judgment requires a nuanced appreciation of
the details of a situation that cannot be reduced to a set of rules.

The debate between Sunnyside Gold Corporation and the State
of Colorado over the environmental consequences of closing the Sunnyside is shot through with such acts of judgment. Take, for instance, the question of why the remediation of the "A" sites in the
basin has not improved the water quality at monitoring site A72
below Silverton. There are any number of possible explanations for
this fact—if, indeed, it is a fact. (The monitoring program itself, for
one reason or another, could be in error.) But assume that the monitoring data are correct; the period of time used as the standard for
judging water quality could be aberrant, a reflection of unusual climatic conditions that affected the degree of heavy metal loading. Or
the current period may be unusual, skewing the readings. It is also
possible that the hydrology of the areas has not yet responded to the
changes—it might well take years or even decades for the effects of
the cleanup to register at A72.

When these points are brought up, field scientists often apolo-
gize for the fundamentally interpretive nature of their research.
After all, "professional judgment" sounds suspiciously like "subjectivity." Such an appeal flies in the face of our culture's image of science, which is supposed to offer a precise and certain basis for policy
decisions. Field sciences such as botany, ecology, hydrology, and geology are thus typically seen as poor kin to laboratory sciences,

which promise reliable (that is, repeatable) results. What goes unappreciated is the fact that such "lab results" are themselves unreal. The variability that a field scientist confronts is the variability of the real world. Faced with such variability, field scientists have developed their skills at making sense out of the hints contained in the rocks or the streams. In philosophy, hermeneutics, or interpretation theory, describes those types of reasoning that rely as much upon experience and discernment as on the ability to calculate.

The question of the nature of field reasoning and its supposed inferiority to the laboratory sciences is a topic of a later chapter. The point here is this: science is typically brought into political controversies because it is seen as the means of resolving debates. The conflict between Sunnyside Gold and the State of Colorado was going to be mediated on the basis of "sound science." Instead, the science itself has become a bone of considerable contention.

But is it possible that we have misled ourselves? Might the entire argument have gone off track? What difference does it make whether the streams of the upper Animas are stressed as a result of mining, or "polluted" by naturally occurring springs and seeps? A pH of 3.2 is a pH of 3.2 in either case.[18] This question is seldom faced head-on, but it hovers about the topic like swamp gas. To address it takes us beyond the discourses of politics and science to subjects that are rarely taken seriously in our environmental debates.

3

CORROSIVE EFFECTS:
ENVIRONMENTAL ETHICS
AND THE METAPHYSICS OF
ACID MINE DRAINAGE

It is clear to all that there is greater detriment from
mining than the value of the metals which the mining
produces.

—Agricola, *De Re Metallica* (1556)

I.

Drill, blast, crush, and scrape: extracting minerals from the
Earth is a brutal business. Even before the machine age, the effects
of mining were transparent: in the *Metamorphoses* (A.D. 7) Ovid
yearned for a lost golden age on Earth before men "dug into her vi-
tals," and Seneca described the results of mining as "a sight to make
hair stand on end."[1] Two thousand years later, Roman mines still poi-
son Italian streams. These effects will not disappear with the development of a postindustrial economy. As long as mining continues,
cyanide spills, acid drainage, and heavy metals contamination will
persist worldwide. And, as the Roman example tells us, these are
problems that outlive the life span of civilizations.

In the summer of 1997, the U.S. Environmental Protection
Agency and the Colorado Division of Public Health and Environment sponsored a conference entitled "Acid Mine Drainage: Problems and Solutions." As the director of the Southwest Earth Studies
Program—a program funded for three years by the National Science

Foundation—I jumped at the chance to attend with my students. The conference was quite informative, hosting exhaustive debates on the scientific dimensions of the controversy over abandoned mine lands and polluted streams. But the most important lesson we took away from the conference had nothing to do with the science of acid mine drainage. Rather, it concerned the way we framed our environmental debates. It started with an offhand remark by one of our students.

A notice for the conference read: "A special effort will be made to involve local citizens in the discussions," but the conference consisted of dauntingly technical presentations. Students' eyes glazed over as mining company officials, remediation experts, and government scientists debated the fine points of the science of remediation. We spent the third and last day of the conference in the field, visiting old mines and remediation sites. At Longfellow-Koehler (a mine site at Red Mountain Pass, at eleven thousand feet in the San Juan Mountains) scientists gathered their data from foul-colored, half-frozen ponds, the numbers flying:

"The pH is 3.45."

"Conductivity is 1120 at this end."

Off to one side, Clark stood with his classmates. Casting a dubious eye upon the proceedings, he leaned over to another student and whispered, "Ah, I don't know. It just looks like sin up here."

Clark's remark, with its seemingly naive appeal to Christian theology, stood in stark contrast to the techno-mathematical discourse of the scientists and engineers. Certainly, the remark could be dismissed as a throwaway comment. But it can also be taken as an authentic response to the environmental degradation before us. Clark's reaction to the polluted site was to fall back upon the theological notion of sin. Later, when his words were brought up in class, Clark received some genial teasing, and he backed away from the remark. It seemed, however, that he had expressed the missing aspect of the debate, the metaphysical or theological kernel of acid mine drainage hidden within a techno-scientific shell. But if this comment exemplifies many people's intuitive response to environmental problems, it is usually expressed in a whisper.

Our environmental debates have gone off track. We are both the victims and the perpetrators of a kind of intellectual bait and switch. We are lured into environmental debates by one set of intuitions, only to find our interests redescribed in terms that are intellectually more respectable. Whole ranges of perspectives—metaphysical, ontological, theological, and aesthetic—find no home within our conversations about nature. Our most heartfelt concerns with environmental degradation are converted into discourses foreign to their origin.

There is evidence that this process of bait and switch is occurring within the upper Animas River watershed. In local acid mine drainage debates, concerns with human health have played a minor role. Silverton draws its drinking water from the Boulder and Bear Creek drainages, which were withdrawn from mineral entry in the nineteenth century. By the time the Animas River reaches larger towns downstream (Durango and Farmington) the flow of heavy metals has been diluted enough to not be a concern.[2] The scant epidemiological research conducted in the Silverton area has not revealed any health problems resulting from the mines.[3] Neither are people making a case in terms of environmental justice—local residents viewing themselves as the victims of a despoiled landscape. The residents of Silverton choose to live there in the face of both economic and meteorological hardships, and are proud of the mining heritage that surrounds them. Finally, if economics were the primary motivation for cleaning up the area's streams (in order to improve either the scenery or the fishing), then it would be more effective to stop all the research and remediation and simply write a check to the citizens of Silverton.

What, then, is the purpose of all the science being done in the Animas drainage? The commonplace answer is that we are gathering the facts needed in order to follow the dictates of the law. The Clean Water Act mandates that we repair the damage done by mining—to "restore the physical, chemical, and biological integrity of the nation's streams." The issue here is determining how much of the acid mine drainage is natural, and how much anthropogenic. But which of our interests are served by distinguishing between the natural and the human-caused? And what would be the point of restoring the streams in these mountains, when so many of them are naturally acidic?

Consider the following two statements describing the current state of environmental debates:

- science is the source of authoritative answers to questions of public policy; and,

- environmental ethics dominates discussions of environmental value.

Both of these statements are rooted in the same soil—the hidden metaphysical assumptions underlying modern culture. We are heirs to a two-hundred-year epistemological prejudice decreeing that certain topics are inadmissible in public debate. We are thus forced to search, often in vain, for scientific, epidemiological, economic, or legal arguments that match the intuitions that we dare not voice.

This chapter offers an account of the relation between these two statements—the dominance of science and the narrowing of environmental philosophy. It also reviews other recent attempts to expand the conversation within environmental philosophy—the environmental justice movement, and ecofeminism. In the end, it returns to the topic of acid mine drainage to explore the metaphysical and theological dimensions of this controversy that have been marginalized.

II.

Science fails to resolve our policy debates, but not because it has nothing to offer. On the contrary, science makes vital contributions by drawing parameters around a problem—eliminating some accounts and suggesting others—and by identifying possible scenarios for the future. But scientific research rarely dictates our behavior, and it cannot substitute for political debate. Science and politics operate within two different language games that rely upon different tools and aim at different ends. The goal of science is a specifically defined—the German philosopher Heidegger would say enframed—notion of truth pursued through controlled experimentation. The goals of politics are, or should be, justice and the common good, pursued through the arts of conversation and compromise.

Daniel Sarewitz expands upon the disjunction between the aims of science and those of politics by noting that, from the point of view of politics, science provides us with an *excess* of objectivity.[4] Sarewitz doesn't question the objectivity of scientific data; in fact, he has little patience for postmodern critics of science who see science as merely a form of ideology. Rather, he highlights another problem: science today is so rich and diverse that it is able to provide support for a wide range of perspectives on a subject. On complex issues like global climate change or the causes of the salmon's decline in the Northwest, science seldom speaks with one voice.

Consider the controversy over salmon. Different parties to the controversy can each point to recent scientific studies that support their own interpretations regarding which of the four Hs (hydropower [dams], habitat degradation, hatchery misuse, and over-harvesting) have caused the drastic decline in salmon populations. Invariably, the debate turns to questions of how to interpret the data, or to claims about the political motivations underlying decisions about scientific methodology.[5] (We have seen the same result in the mine controversy over acid mine drainage, where competing hydrologists have offered strikingly different models of the results of flooding the Sunnyside mine.) In the words of one of the researchers involved with the salmon controversy, "Science can provide us with information about choices, but it is not going to deliver the Holy Grail."[6]

But more than the failure of science to solve our controversies, the basic issue is this: neither the calculus of science and economics, nor the interest-group orientation of contemporary politics, can express the heart of our concerns about environmental degradation. A lifeless, foul-smelling river excites our disgust, but we turn to the chemist and the public health official to define our outrage. The cutting of old growth forests elicits a sense of loss, but we ask the ecologist and economist to quantify these losses. The feebleness of this approach is apparent as soon as we examine our own reactions to environmental destruction. We are sickened by a fouled stream even if our water supply is located elsewhere; and converting an ancient forest into stacks of 2×4s evokes, in many, a sense of sacrilege. Our most heartfelt concerns have been converted into foreign discourses, the languages of science, economics, and interest-group politics.

In the *Ethics,* Aristotle makes a point about the nature of reasoning that helps us clarify this issue. Aristotle emphasizes the importance of distinguishing between arguments *to* and arguments *from* first principles. We don't reason our way *to* the conclusion that inflicting gratuitous pain upon children is evil; rather, we begin *from* the intuition that this is wrong, and seek an account of ethics that explains it. Any ethics trying to demonstrate the reasonableness of torturing toddlers would strike us as more than a little mad. Intuition may seem a weak reed upon which to base our environmental claims, but we all begin our thinking with one intuition or another. Science itself is based upon intuitions that can never be fully demonstrated— for instance, that the universe is an orderly place, that our senses (mostly) do not lie, or that we can adequately analogize from controlled conditions to the real world. Without these basic intuitions our thinking is lost in an infinite regress, as we are forced to demonstrate the premises of each of our conclusions, then the premises of those premises, ad infinitum. This does not, however, imply a retreat into dogmatism. What keeps intuitions from becoming dogmatic is our willingness to submit them to public debate, allowing them to be informed by both evidence and differing intuitions.

What, then, are our intuitions or first principles concerning environmental controversies such as acid mine drainage? Are we reasoning *to* a conclusion that we are unaware of, or *from* an insight that already resonates deeply within us? It seems clear that in some cases we are reasoning from an insight rather than to a conclusion. In the 1960s, the proposed dams in the Grand Canyon struck many as wrong, not chiefly because of scientific or economic arguments concerning the poor returns on investment or the dangers of catastrophic failure, but because the dams would despoil a natural wonder. If this intuition lies at the heart of our concern with the Grand Canyon (or with the salmon, or at the Longfellow-Koehler mine), then why aren't such metaphysical or theological intuitions appropriate within our environmental debates?

Serious consideration of either of these topics has been enjoined for two hundred years. Across philosophy, and more generally throughout intellectual culture, metaphysics and theology have been dismissed as retrograde and irrational. Here I invoke the terms metaphysics and theology in a minimalist fashion—arguing for the pertinence of that which is beyond the material or physical (meta-physics), as well as for the widespread sense of reverence elicited by tremendous landscapes. This is in clear contrast to the stance of dogmatic metaphysics and theology, which base themselves in unverifiable, unquestionable truth claims and remain closed to reform or evolution. This essay takes a phenomenological approach: rather than admitting only legalisms or testable realities to public debate, it also honors claims based in the experience of the natural and the sacred. This approach places intuitions in dialectical relation with other views, and is open to reformation by either scientific facts or other intuitions.

My claim, then, is that our relation with the natural world is as much rooted in metaphysical and theological intuitions as it is in the intricacies of scientific or ethical debate. In this sense, a metaphysically or theologically oriented environmentalism is also a deeply practical environmentalism. But before exploring our intuitions concerning acid mine drainage, we need to account for the general silence of environmental philosophy on these questions.[7]

III.

Environmental philosophy is a young discipline: its leading journal, *Environmental Ethics,* was not founded until 1979. The field's origins are straightforward, at least in outline: Rachel Carson's *Silent Spring* forcefully brought environmental degradation to the public's attention in 1962, and Senator Gaylord Nelson sponsored the first Earth Day in 1970. Spurred by these concerns, academic philosophers began exploring the possibility of a distinctively environmental ethic. Baird Callicott taught what might have been the first course in environmental ethics in 1971, at the University of Wisconsin, Stevens Point. And in 1975, Holmes Rolston III's essay, "Is There an Ecological Ethic?" appeared in the journal *Ethics*.[8]

The beginnings of environmental philosophy did, however, contain a theoretical presumption. The birth of environmental philosophy of the 1970s represents a break from the classic questions of the Western tradition of natural philosophy. Across its many variations, this two-thousand-year tradition had continued from Thales (sixth century B.C.) through the nineteenth century German idealists Hegel and Schelling. With Schelling's death in 1854, natural philosophy turned into the philosophy of science. It was a momentous shift: philosophy no longer sought the purpose of our lives within the processes of the natural world. Now the scientific method provided our only rational access to the world, with natural philosophy and theology passing into the shadows. And the scientific method revealed only a physical world driven by blind causes.

To highlight what was at stake in this shift from natural philosophy to the philosophy of science, it is perhaps more useful to refer to the former as *cosmology*, for its goal was to identify humanity's proper place in the *cosmos* or universe. Greek philosophy was founded on the assumption that there was an order *(logos)* to the world, and this order expressed the purpose inherent in all things. It was the role of philosophy to identify this purpose. One of the upshots of this effort was ethical: by discovering the purpose of the universe, we would simultaneously reveal the characteristics of the good life. To put the point differently, the main concern of natural philosophy was not with what we call *nature* (rocks, animals, ecosystems), but with the *natural*. The natural order of things possessed prescriptive and proscriptive force: the way things were implied the way things were supposed to be. Thus Plato, Aristotle, and the Stoic philosophers all called upon us to pattern our lives on the *logos* surrounding us.

For the vast majority of thinkers over the next two thousand years, the natural order was simultaneously a metaphysical and a moral order: the individual and human society were microcosms to be modeled upon the macrocosm of nature. Humankind sought principles for how to live—that is, an ethics—and ethics would find its basis in an understanding of the basic purpose of the universe. This last concern fell within the domain of metaphysics—literally, the investigations that Aristotle pursued after the *Physics*. Aristotle called these questions "first philosophy" because while ethics was the fulfillment of philosophic insight, the principles that grounded our ethics must be sought for elsewhere.

This tradition died at the hands of modernism. The philosophers of modern science—Bacon, Descartes, Galileo, Newton—described a world devoid of purpose: only efficient or mechanical causes rather than final ones existed. Of course, it took a while for this message to take hold. Natural theology flourished through the eighteenth century in the form of the argument from design. To William Paley, for example, the natural world exhibited an order that could only be explained by referring to a creative intelligence. In the mid-nineteenth century, Darwin's theory of natural selection would put an end to such reasoning by offering a nonteleological explanation of biologic adaptations. By placing human beings firmly within an aimless natural order, Darwin left us as purposeless as the merest molecules.[9] But even before the death of natural theology, philosophers were seeking a noncosmological basis for ethics—Kant in the ethical implications of pure reasoning, Bentham and Mill in pleasure and pain. For all their differences, what united these theories was the sense that there was no point in looking to nature for a normative principle. Nature modeled nothing except utter randomness. Physics and ethics, the material universe and the good life, lost their connection.

More recently, the loss of nature as a normative principle has encouraged a proceduralist approach to ethics. No longer having rational access to what is right, the right has become whatever results from following a set of rules. Contemporary ethics means engaging in the proper process, rather than the training and cultivating of the soul. It is the triumph of process over results. Once we deny the possibility of identifying a common good to our lives, all that remains are rules and procedures. The question of what constitutes the good life is now a private issue—private by default, because the question is not subject to rational debate.

Contrast this with the Greeks, for whom the term *ethos* meant habituating oneself to a set of virtues (e.g., courage, magnanimity, loyalty). The difference is apparent in Plato's *Republic*. Socrates seeks to describe the just individual and the just city, a discussion concerned with what we would call ethics. But to address these concerns, Socrates turns not to questions of rights and obligations, but

to music. His musical definition of justice emphasizes the importance of being properly attuned, both within the self (not too rash,
not too timid) and in one's relations to others. The melody or tone of
a conversation is as important as the lyrics (that is, the propositions)
uttered, and society is seen as a symphony within which everyone
plays the part proper to them. This is a strikingly different conception of ethics from today's rule-driven debates.

By the twentieth century, then, the modernist stance toward
nature had become the received wisdom within both the university
and the culture at large. The result was that environmental philosophy would be cast in terms of environmental ethics—even if
environmental debates regularly strained the bounds of this desig-
nation. The physical world was brute matter devoid of purpose, a
world that science could in principle fully describe. Metaphysics,
aesthetics, and theology were antiquated categories that had lost
their raison d'être, and were now seen as simple expressions of dogmatism and subjectivity. In the 1960s, when environmental issues
caught the attention of the public, these concerns were naturally
expressed in the two languages most likely to get a hearing: science,
which defined the real, and ethics, which addressed questions of
rights and obligations. By default, environmental philosophy became environmental ethics. Ethics may have been as subjective as
these other discredited fields, but it still retained a degree of importance, for people are always jealous to protect their rights. John
Passmore summarized the state of affairs within environmental
philosophy in the title of his book (one of the first book-length treat-
ments of environmental philosophy), *Man's Responsibility for
Nature* (1974). Passmore argued that we could not have any responsibility *to* the brute, aimless material that is nature. Our only
responsibility was to guard against nature becoming the medium of
injustice to our fellow citizens, say through the improper use of natural resources.

We must not caricature environmental philosophy's current situation. To take one example, within the journal *Environmental
Ethics* we find an impressively wide range of topics, including environmental policy, politics, aesthetics, metaphysics, and theology.
Furthermore, environmental philosophy hasn't entirely abandoned
metaphysical and theological perspectives. It is a commonplace
within the field to contrast the approaches to nature of Gifford Pinchot and John Muir—Pinchot is seen as representing the utilitarian
position, while Muir is seen as a religious mystic whose defense of
nature is grounded in pantheism.[10] On this account, a metaphysical

or theological perspective lies at the roots of one of the two main currents of environmental philosophy. Similarly, the debate between anthropocentrism and biocentrism, possibly the most rehearsed argument within environmental philosophy, is fundamentally an argument about nature's metaphysical status. Biocentrism is often described as a religious or metaphysical commitment, and the question of identifying nature's value as having a nonhuman origin has given birth to hundreds of essays and monographs.

Nevertheless, ethics still controls the discussion on philosophy's contribution to environmental debates. "Environmental ethics" dominates the titles of articles, books, journals, and conferences. Of course, one may reply, these are only *titles,* but titles frame the logical space of the conversation. When such examples can be multiplied (as they can within environmental philosophy), individual instances begin to form a larger pattern: ethics rules our environmental conversations, muting other perspectives. While these other perspectives are present, they are sufficiently muffled so that, for most outsiders, environmental philosophy and environmental ethics are synonymous.

Environmental philosophers are responding to the presumption of our culture at large, whose definition of the real is limited to the results of the scientific method and the legalistic discourse of rights and obligations. The intellectual classes, whether scientific or humanistic, have not taken metaphysics and theology—much less aesthetics—seriously since the Enlightenment. But if environmental philosophy is going to make a greater contribution to culture than it has to date, we must find a way to expand our culture's dialogue on the environment to include these aspects of our response to the natural world.

IV.

In recent years it is possible to discern a shift in the center of gravity within environmental philosophy. The environmental justice movement and ecofeminism represent two innovations in environmental thinking.

The environmental justice movement aims to correct environmentalism's traditional disregard of our built environments. It criticizes the traditional focus of environmental ethics upon wilderness preservation and endangered species, which it sees as evidence that environmental ethics is out of touch with the lives and concerns of most people today. Instead, these authors and activists take up environmental issues that manifest themselves in our cities, suburbs, and rural countryside. But despite this shift in focus, the environmental justice movement goes no farther than environmental ethics in taking metaphysics and theology seriously.

Advocates of environmental justice analyze how environmental risks are distributed through communities, and seek policies that equalize who shoulders these burdens. In 1995, the U.S. General Accounting Office estimated that some 450,000 sites in the United States qualify as "brownfields"—abandoned industrial sites that must be cleaned up before they are suitable for new uses. Not surprisingly, brownfields are disproportionately located in areas where minorities and low-income groups live. Advocates of environmental justice not only address questions of where dirty industries, incinerators, and waste dumps are sited, but also suburban sprawl and the loss of open space, the role of citizens or "stakeholders" groups in the framing of environmental policies, and the possible dangers of genetically modified food ("frankenfood").

Part of the reason environmental justice advocates put less emphasis upon the preservation of pristine nature is that they see it as a dubious category. Our influence upon the land, the seas, and the ice caps has been so pervasive that some authors speak of the "end of nature."[11] Instead, environmental justice focuses on two issues: the aforementioned concern with distributive justice, and the question of how to restore lands that have been damaged through human activity or neglect. It is this second point, the philosophic questions surrounding restoring lands damaged by human actions or neglect, that is our concern here. Of course, not all of these compromised sites are in developed areas. Some are in relatively wild places like the San Juan Mountains. It is here that the clash of perspectives among environmentalists becomes most clamorous.

The question of how—or whether—to repair damaged landscapes prompts a wide spread of reactions. Some environmental philosophers find the very idea of restoring nature offensive. Eric Katz is concerned that the ability to restore damaged landscapes undercuts the argument for preserving unspoiled places. Katz also sees ecological restoration as a sign of our arrogance toward the natural world, expressing the ideology that as the masters and possessors of nature, we are free to manipulate the entire world to suit our desires.[12] In a similar vein, Bruce V. Foltz objects to transforming the science of ecology from a descriptive science into a predictive and manipulative one. He sees this shift as another step in the direction

of turning the sciences into fundamentally technological exercises—
their goal being not so much to know the world, but to control and
manipulate it.[13]

In contrast, researchers and working scientists and technicians within the field of ecological restoration often fail to see anything wrong with intervening in the restoration of compromised
landscapes. These commentators view the development of restoration techniques as a wholly positive sign of our increasing technological prowess to achieve our desires.[14] Restoration is simply
another example of what we do best. As technological beings, we
naturally fashion the world to suit our wishes. In this case, we
want to put the environment back into something approximating
its original state.

A related perspective rejects the very concept of "restoring" the
environment. Brad Allenby, an engineer and vice president of AT&T,
claims that natural systems have been so affected by our activities
that the Earth itself has become an artifact. Not only has every
ecosystem from the tropics to the Arctic been affected by human activity. We also find signs of millennial-old copper smelting in Green-
land's ice cores, and atmospheric CO_2 has been rising for millennia
as we have deforested Europe and Asia. Talk of minimizing or re-
versing our impacts implies the false belief in the retrievability of a
prior, pure natural state.

> The issue is not whether we should *begin* ESEM [Earth Sci-
> ence Engineering and Management], because we have been
> doing that for a long time, albeit unintentionally in many
> cases. Rather, the issue is whether we will assume the ethi-
> cal responsibilities to do ESEM rationally and responsibly.[15]

Allenby calls for us to recognize our responsibility for administering
the Earth, and inaugurate a self-conscious program of planetary engineering and management. We must abandon anachronistic ap-
peals to nature, and recognizing our responsibility to manage the
environment for "maximum functionality."[16]

Still another position, advanced by Chris Maser and others, focuses on the process rather than on the result of restoring damaged
landscapes. Participating in the actual work of restoration offers us
the chance to build a more harmonious relationship with nature:

> The very process of restoring the land to health is the
> process through which we become attuned with Nature, and,

through Nature, with ourselves. Restoration, therefore, is both the means and the end, for as we learn how to restore the land, we heal the ecosystem, and as we heal the ecosystem, we heal ourselves.[17]

Restoring the land becomes the means for overcoming the dualism that opposes human activity to the natural world. Restoration work is seen as creating an intimate relationship similar to that the farmer, or, as we will see, the field scientist. Other writers have taken this point a step further, claiming that the chief reason for restoring damaged landscapes is not natural but political. Carolyn Merchant and Andrew Light draw attention to the importance of volunteer labor in ecological restoration, where citizens, rather than scientists or technicians, play a leading role. They view the restoration process as a political act; the effort to restore the land unites the community and strengthens people's democratic impulses.[18]

Ecofeminism presents us with a second prominent development within environmental philosophy. Françoise d'Eaubonne introduced the term "l'eco-féminisme" in 1974, thereby announcing the emergence of the environment as a feminist issue.[19] D'Eaubonne argued that both overpopulation and the destruction of natural resources have their source in society's phallocentric order—that is, in the historical, conceptual, and symbolic perspectives typical of men. For d'Eaubonne, the subjugation of women's reproductive power has led to overpopulation, while the domination of the natural world has led to the current environmental crisis. In a similar vein, Rosemary Radford Ruether has argued: "Women must see that there can be no liberation for them and no solution to ecological crisis within a society whose fundamental model of relationships continues to be one of domination."[20] Ruether's goal is to effect a cultural transformation within society, away from the masculine-coded values of possession, conquest, and accumulation, and toward the feminine-coded values of reciprocity, harmony, and interdependence.

Ecofeminists have claimed that applying the Western development model within non-Western nations has led to policies that negatively impact women's lives, and that environmental health risks weigh more heavily upon women than men. They have also focused on the distinctive nature of women's spirituality, emphasizing the relation that indigenous women have to the Earth.[21] Nor have these speculations been confined to theorizing: Chris Cuomo and

Stephanie Lahar have emphasized that activism and grassroots politics are the necessary corollary to any theory.[22]

In highlighting the plight of women worldwide and the ties between the situation of women and the natural environment, ecofeminist theory faces two challenges. First is the difficulty of parsing the claim that the problems faced by women and the environment are rooted in "phallocentrism," i.e., in attitudes typical of men. Second is the question of whether it is appropriate to simply condemn the list of these attributes.

To date, ecofeminism lacks a convincing account of the nature of human selfhood as being overwhelmingly determined by gender, as well as an account of how the category of gender applies to individual women and men. When someone acts or speaks, how can we tell whether they do so out of their sexual orientation, economic interest, ethnic background, regional background, social class, economic class, age, or any of the other myriad parts of the self? The motivation behind our behavior may be based in any (or any combination) of these interests. Without a persuasive account of how to parse this point, it begs the question to refer to any particular act of domination as "phallocentric." Rather than in the purported masculine orientation of culture, acts of domination may simply be rooted in the fact that humans are ill-tempered creatures who will oppress whomever they can—other races, cultures, religions, or genders. Ecofeminists are thus open to the charge of commiting a non sequitur—that so-called ecofeminist strategies of multiplicity, diversity, and reciprocity have no particular connection to either women or men. One can be quite sympathetic to feminist concerns, and quite concerned about the environment, while still doubting that ecofeminists have made a compelling case for a deep connection between the two.

But let us assume for a moment that the argument has been made that there is a deep connection between masculine attitudes, the oppression of women, and our current environmental concerns. If men are more aggressive and dominating in nature, are these characteristics that should simply be condemned? In the *Republic*, Socrates speaks of the importance of the virtue of *thymos*, the anger or spiritedness of the warrior. Are there no situations where such a response is appropriate? After all, some feminists defended the virtues of the warrior, that is, U.S. military intervention, in response to the systematic rape of Bosnian Muslim and Croat women in the late 1990s. Environmental activist Julia "Butterfly" Hill lived in a two-hundred-foot-tall redwood tree from 10 December 1997 to

18 December 1999, in a forest 230 miles north of San Francisco. We may, of course, read this act in a variety of ways; but one plausible description would see this as the manifestation of the warrior spirit in defense of the ancient redwood forest. Ecofeminism has rarely acknowledged that there are virtues as well as vices involved in typically masculine attitudes—that what we need in our attitudes toward nature as toward culture, is an artful mix of stereotypically feminine and masculine virtues, as Socrates argued about the guardian class. A thorough ecofeminism would thus be an ecofeminism that would be at the same time an ecomasculinism.

In sum, neither environmental justice nor ecofeminism speaks to the metaphysical or theological intuition ("it just looks like sin") voiced that day at Longfellow-Koehler. So let us return to the case of acid mine drainage. Assume that the conclusions reached by scientists to date are correct—that more than half of the water "pollution" in the San Juans is natural, arising from geologic conditions that predate mining.[23] Many of these streams have been lifeless since the end of the last ice age (and before that, buried beneath the ice!). But if a stream is naturally abiotic, do we leave it alone, and reclaim only those rivers that have been affected by our actions? Or should our goal be to introduce fish into all the streams?

Put the question another way: say the goal is to reduce contamination to the point where fish can live in the Cement Creek drainage. We find that two major sources of pollution add approximately equal amounts of acidified water and heavy metals to the creek: a natural iron bog that runs alongside the road, and an old mine halfway up the mountainside. The mine, being less accessible and more geologically complex, will be twice as expensive to clean as the iron bog. Why not clean up the iron bog, letting the human-affected site stand in its place? After all, there is no physical difference between a naturally occurring sulfur ion and a human-produced one (GL:CH3).

But might there be a metaphysical difference? That is, could there be a reason to leave the naturally lifeless streams alone, only restoring those that we have damaged? Or a reason for spending more money to remediate the mine halfway up the mountain, leaving the natural iron bog as it is? Does it even make sense to speak of "restoring" nature, or would the result of these efforts simply be a Disney-like imitation of what once was there?

Within environment debates, Robert Elliott's *Faking Nature* perhaps comes closest to addressing these concerns.[24] Elliott's interest is in what he calls restoration's ontological aspects. What is at stake if a mining company can completely restore an area after the mining is completed, to the point that no one can tell the difference afterward?[25] Elliott argues that such a re-created landscape is comparable to a forged painting. Even if the copy can't be distinguished from the original, something essential has been lost.

That something is the land's origin and peculiar history. For not only is the land's physical constitution important to us, but so too is its ontological status. Elliott offers us the analogy of a beautiful, handcrafted knife received as a gift. We cherish the knife and display it prominently in our home. We then discover that the gift was fashioned from the bone of a person killed expressly for the purpose of making the knife. This knowledge changes none of the knife's chemical or physical characteristics. Nonetheless, its nature has been irretrievably altered; the knife is now a source of horror rather than delight. The knife's *meaning* has changed. Similarly, a reconstructed landscape or ecosystem might match the land's original condition, down to the last detail. Nevertheless, the reconstruction would lack the meaning inherent in the original landscape. The unique origin and history of the land would have been destroyed, and we would be left with a human artifact.

By focusing on the question of meaning, Elliott opens the door to a phenomenological interpretation of our experience of nature. But is the analogy of a restored landscape to a work of art—fake or not—appropriate? The problem with this analogy is that it ignores the difference between nature and human creations. For the Greeks, *phusis* identified the realm of self-organizing nature; *technê,* the artifactual world of human-created objects. Describing restored nature by way of an analogy to a (faked) work of art thus misses precisely what is distinctive about nature: its fundamental otherness, the fact that it has an internal dynamic all its own, both before and after it has been restored.[26] While artifacts are passive, nature is recalcitrant. Even if we reconstruct the land in accordance with our wishes, nature soon heads off in its own direction. (This is a constant problem in restoration projects, as the remediated site is likely to stop functioning in way we intended, instead reaching a new state of its own creating.) In this sense, we can speak of a restored landscape regaining its naturalness, as it slowly reasserts its *phusis*. In contrast, the artifact has no internal principle of ordering that directs its development. The only way it asserts its naturalness is by breaking down.

Nonetheless, Elliott has opened a trail that we can follow further. Let us turn, then, to a fuller account of the metaphysics and theology of acid mine drainage.

V.

... an act that evolves an evil, an impurity, a fluid, a mysterious and harmful something that acts dynamically—that is to say, magically.

—Pettazzoni, *La confession des péchés* (1931)

The exotic carries its own peculiar certification, just as familiarity breeds, if not contempt, then nonchalance and a kind of blindness. In an age governed by the notion of *Homo economicus*— the belief that our interests are fundamentally self-interested and consumerist in orientation—is it possible to treat the statement "It looks like sin" seriously? Can a young man's comment be seen as an expression of an experience of transcendence, similar to how phenomenologist of religion Mircea Eliade interprets the myths of the Kwakiutl, or the philosopher Paul Ricoeur the symbolism of poetry or dreams? Of course, this is to conflate the great with the small—the glittering traditions of world religions with a student's offhand remark. But how, then, are we to interpret the behavior of the millions who each year make pilgrimages to natural shrines such as the Grand Canyon and Yellowstone? Should the ongoing work at Summitville, 150 million dollars of public monies spent to remediate an obscure location high in the Rockies, be understood as the logical result following the dictates of science, or as an act of atonement?

Defilement is a category from a bygone era: we have lost the capacity to treat notions of stain and infection as objective reports of our being. But might these intuitions live on as subterranean influences, reappearing in the passive voices of scientific papers? When Ricoeur identifies the two elements of defilement as infection by an obscure "something," and dread of a looming retribution that bears down upon us, it is not difficult to see how these points may be pertinent to contemporary environmental dramas like acid mine drainage.[27] Environmental concern may well become the organizing principle of civilization, as Al Gore suggested in 1993, but this does not preclude our interpreting the apocalyptic tones of much environmental rhetoric—what Theodore Roszak has called "guilt trips and scare tactics"—as expressions of the symbolism of evil.[28]

Invoking the sacred and its transgression in relation to environmental degradation does not imply an exclusively Christian perspective on environmental harm. Sin, transgression, and atonement are concepts that transcend individual cultures. On the basis of his historical and cultural studies, Eliade claims that the sacred is a purely formal category: "The first possible definition of the *sacred* is that it is *the opposite of the profane*."[29] By this he means that rather than referring to a particular object—a shell, a stone, or a grove of trees—the sacred expresses absolute difference, the bare idea of limit, boundary, and otherness.[30] It manifests itself through an initial break in experience that provides us with an orientation in life— a boundary in cultural space that prescribes and proscribes, and thus provides the basis of any ethics. The sacred expresses our sense that there must be bounds to human behavior, and without such boundaries our lives lack meaning and purpose.

Paul Ricoeur holds that consciousness of sin depends upon a prior establishment of a covenant; sin implies the shattering of the bond between man and God. Ricoeur therefore suggests that the notion of sin presupposes a theistic element—either monotheistic or polytheistic. But this is an unnecessary stipulation: nature itself has an order that makes claims upon us. So, for instance, in *Oedipus Rex,* Oedipus's *hubris* violates natural limits that exist beyond or outside of any explicitly established covenant. The sacred is the *ganz andere* (wholly other) revealed through a hierophany, a break in space or a surpassing of a threshold or limit, that in the first instance shows itself in nature: in mountains, forests, or bodies of water.[31] The sacred is thus identified with something more elemental and intuitive, and much less doctrinal, than what usually falls under the heading of "religion." It is the intuition that expresses itself in our horror at the defacing of the petroglyph known as the Moab Panel at Arches National Park in 1981.

Today, a chorus of voices—including many in the environmental movement—reject out of hand an appeal to the sacred, whether in relation to environmental questions or to any other public issue. For some, associations with religious fundamentalism and right-wing politics have fatally compromised the discussion of such perspectives. (Seldom remarked upon is the fact that much of the motivation behind the Civil Rights movement of the 1960s was religious in nature.) The introduction of the sacred in public discourse is commonly rebuffed by referring to the Establishment Clause of the First Amendment: "Congress shall make no law respecting an establishment of religion, or prohibiting the free exercise thereof." But this misleads the debate. The authors of the Constitution were not interested in eliminating religion from public life—only in preventing the establishment of one church over all others. More to the point here, the lived experience of the sacred is distinct from questions about the place of organized, doctrinal religion in public life.

The sacred calls us to acknowledge and honor the otherness of nature. It renounces the egotism demanding that the entire world speak our name. The sacred implies the centrality of the notion of care—the capacity to restrain oneself, to control one's desires in order to make space for another. Only then can another being manifest its own nature through the process of self-emergence that the Greeks called *phusis*. *Phusis* and care provide us with another, nonhuman-centered standard for measuring our environmental responsibilities. Placing care at the center of an environmental metaphysics or theology offers us a criterion other than that of pH and conductivity for approaching the problems of acid mine drainage.

What should we clean up, and to what degree? Those areas that display a lack of care. A painstakingly woven wooden trellis-works supporting an old mineworks; the remains of a mill's carefully worked stone foundation, left by an avalanche that hit in the winter of '52; a miner's bunkhouse hanging precariously at eleven thousand feet, reachable only by an arduous hike: these places embody the labors, the dangers, and the nobility of the miner's life, and should be preserved—or perhaps allowed to weather, age, and eventually decay of their own accord. In contrast, the heaps of rusting corrugated sheet metal and scattered pipes dumped along the side of a jeep road, and the bright ooze leaking from an old mine shaft—such wanton carelessness we clean up, restoring the area to a semblance of its former condition. The point of such restoration isn't to eliminate all signs of wear and tear, but rather to get nature started on its way toward healing itself (GL:CH3).

As for the streams: clean up the mounds of mine tailings dumped in the rivers, and correct the worst of our desecrations, such as the violent mounds of gravel left along the Blue River in central Colorado, the legacy of placer mining. Acknowledge the otherness of nature by leaving the natural iron bog, while cleaning up our own depredations—even at additional cost. If hydrologists are clear that a stream was lifeless before miners arrived, let it be. On the other hand, if it appears that a stream held fish before the miners arrived, and that it can be coaxed back to life, let us do so. But if the task would require a reconstruction so massive that it would leave us with something more akin to Disneyland than nature, then let it heal in its own time; over the millennia, nature's own recuperative powers will restore the land. If this seems too slow, let it serve as a reminder of the consequences of our behavior, a defilement that we must live with.

An environmental metaphysics and politics rooted in care does not apply only to questions of ecological restoration. Care can also be shown toward pristine nature, as well as through the improvement of nature. In the case of pristine nature, care is manifested by allowing an area to develop in its own fashion essentially unimpeded—the attitude embodied in the Wilderness Act of 1964.[32] Human activities can also add to a landscape. This is true not only in some cases of mining activity; a well-managed agricultural area can also bring the natural capacities of a region to completion. Care also shows itself via the cultivation of a sacred natural space, such as the Kurama District outside of Kyoto. The trail up to Mt. Kurama passes through dense woods, seemingly in natural condition. Small Buddhist and Shinto temples and shrines that serve as the occasion for reflection and meditation on nature also mark the trail. Near the top of the mountain is the Kurama Buddhist Temple; founded in 770, it serves as a focal point for the mountain. The overall effect is to add to rather than detract from the natural beauty of the area (GL:CH3).

Make no mistake, particular cases of environmental destruction like the Sunnyside, Longfellow-Koehler at Red Mountain Pass, and the Summitville Mine site call for a nuanced, site-specific response rather than a one-size-fits-all answer. Nor should it be thought that metaphysical and theological perspectives can answer all our questions, environmental or otherwise. The geologist, the lawyer, the ethicist, and the economist each have their own, at times decisive, addition to make. Our environmental controversies require a plurality of approaches: environmental science and public policy, environmental ethics and justice, and yes, environmental metaphysics and theology.

VI.

While cast in the languages of science, economics, and interest group politics, our environmental debates are, in truth, caught up in questions of metaphysics, theology, and aesthetics. Metaphysics and theology express our concern with deep real and the sacred, while beauty is the shining of the real, truth become sensuous. Unfortunately, these perspectives are able to gain little traction today, because of an epistemological presumption: reality is defined by those facts discoverable through the processes of the scientific method.

Thus, for all the seeming irrelevance of philosophy in culture, it turns out that our social and political lives depend on philosophic presumptions. For it is our epistemological standards, about what counts as real or "objective," that define the boundaries of thought and conversation. After all, public discussions require some standard for evaluating whether a claim about the nature of reality is not just a figment of an overheated imagination. Politics—that is, our community's dialogue on matters of common concern—depends upon a dialectic of metaphysics and epistemology, a vision of reality tempered by the proof we can offer to support it. Not only our private but also our public lives depend on an agreed-upon sense of what counts as true.

There are signs today that these debates are moving beyond a ritualized dismissal of the sacred.[33] But to make real headway in introducing metaphysical and theological perspectives into our environmental conversations, we must confront the epistemological presumptions that have marginalized them. For it is against the purported clarity and objectivity of scientific knowledge that these other topics are rejected as spurious. The nature and status of scientific knowledge thus become central to evaluating the metaphysical and theological perspectives presented here. We turn, then, to questions of epistemology and the philosophy of science—the gatekeepers of our imagination, as well as of our conversations.

4

THE PLACES OF SCIENCE: THE HEAVENS, THE LAB, THE FIELD, AND THE SCREEN

Science sets the standard for rationality in today's society.

—Steve Fuller

"Epistemology" is one of those words that people have trouble remembering the definition of. When they are reminded that it means "the theory of knowledge," the term calls forth images of philosophers absorbed in obscure debates. The image is accurate enough: we rarely see philosophers of science holding forth on Sunday morning talk shows. Nevertheless, epistemology casts a long shadow upon our public life. Our implicit understanding of what can be known defines the conceptual space of our public conversations. After all, we can hardly debate issues that are fundamentally unknowable—or as we say today, "merely subjective."

Our current understanding of knowledge has defined ethics, politics, aesthetics, theology, and metaphysics as areas where critical judgment is impossible. On these topics we can only share feelings. Since the end of the nineteenth century, we have firmly established science as our culture's exemplar of knowledge. Friedrich Nietzsche vividly expressed science's prominence—and its dangers—in 1882. In *The Gay Science*, the Madman's cry that "God is dead" reflects the fact that claimants to knowledge such as religion had lost their status as sources of a common truth. But rather than endorsing this state of affairs, the parable ends with the question of whether humans can function with only a scientific definition of truth.[1] Of course, the question itself assumes that science is a specially defined domain of knowledge, sharply distinct from other areas.

59

Over the last twenty years, the field of science studies has challenged this assumption. Doing so has led to acrimonious debate. The
debate exerts a strong gravitational pull, drawing in anyone who
questions the standard epistemological account of the sciences.[2] It is
a debate typically cast in terms of polarities—science as unimpeach-
able fact, or as ideological construction. In fact, a broad middle
ground exists that sees science as both a report on reality and as
deeply reflecting various types of values.[3]

The field of science studies has left its mark upon the philosophy of science; while some philosophers remain largely unaffected
(practicing what Giere calls "analytical philosophy in historical
robes"),[4] the range of acceptable interests within the field has expanded. In *The Dappled World,* Nancy Cartwright distinguishes between two different types of philosophy of science. Citing Hacking's
distinction between representing and intervening, Cartwright notes
that philosophers such as Bas van Fraassen are interested in questions such as "How can the world be the way that science says it is or
represents it to be?" Cartwright describes her own interest as "How
can the world be changed by science to make it as it should be?" For
Cartwright, the sciences consist of a series of regional accounts of reality with no clear hierarchy ranking them (i.e., physics does not
"ground" other sciences). She describes the relation between the various disciplines as "here and there, once in a while, corners that line
up, but mostly ragged edges."[5] But Cartwright's own question leaves
a great deal unanswered. It says nothing about the possibility that
science itself may be part of the problem, contributing to the problems we face, or that political, aesthetic, and metaphysical commitments may lie at the heart of science, or that what our society most
needs may lie in those areas of human endeavor associated with the
humanities. Absent these questions, we are left with a badly trun-
cated philosophy of science.

There is also the question of audience. The groups interested in
science today may be roughly divided into four: practicing scientists,
professional students of science (philosophers of science, science policy analysts, historians, and sociologists), undergraduates (whose
knowledge of science largely comes from textbooks), and the general
public. Only the second group has the time to develop a nuanced understanding of how to marry traditional philosophy of science with
science studies. Undergraduate textbooks offer accounts of science
that still hearken to pre-Kuhnian positivism; and to a surprising degree, standard anthologies within the philosophy of science hardly
mention science studies. The public's understanding of science is

largely based on triumphal reports of the latest scientific innovations and discoveries.

Given science's central position in societal debates, careful reflection on its use and misuse—that is, a *philosophy* of science—should occupy a central place in public life. Regrettably, this has not been the case. The philosophy of science has had little or no public presence in interpreting science's status and its relationship to society. The reasons for this are many and varied, but I want to explore one important cause: the role that *examples* have played in defining our culture's understanding of science. Society's understanding of the power *and* limits of science has been inadequate in part because of how science has been portrayed through the use of a few exemplary cases. Relying upon examples of science taken from the heavens and the laboratory, rather than the field, philosophers of science have perpetuated a dangerously unrealistic image of science.

I will develop this point through a brief examination of four classic sites of science: the heavens, the lab, the field, and the computer screen.

I.

In general, nature does not prepare situations to fit the kinds of mathematical theories we hanker for.

—Nancy Cartwright, *How the Laws of Physics Lie*

While philosophers commonly date its beginnings in the Vienna Circle's work of the 1920s, in important ways the field that came to be known as the philosophy of science originated in the 1850s. This was when the William Whewell coined the term "scientist," and when the older tradition of *Naturphilosophie* gave way to the positivist assumptions of Comte. At its birth, this new discipline might have defined its subject in a number of ways. It might have become a branch of political philosophy, studying the effects of scientific discoveries on society, and how science could best contribute to societal aims. Or it could have become a subdivision of epistemology, focusing on the nature of the scientific method, and certifying the status of scientific claims. Or it could have taken up both tasks, grounding the philosophy of science in both political philosophy and epistemology.[6]

The philosophy of science defined its task as being fundamentally epistemological in nature. For 150 years, the discipline has focused on questions concerning induction, prediction, and evidence; models of explanation; the laws of nature; and scientific realism. This choice was itself rooted in the philosophic belief that scientific knowledge was, in its essence, distinct from politics. Science produced objective knowledge, while politics consisted of interest groups struggling for self-advancement. Mixing science and politics was to confuse vastly different categories.

In the last two decades this distinction has broken down, in fact if not in theory, for at least two reasons. First, science has become a cultural presence in its own right. In 2002 federal budget of the United States, funding for non-defense science totaled over 40 billion dollars; the National Institutes of Health alone received 24 billion, the National Science Foundation, nearly 5 billion. Such amounts of money not only support the creation of an enormous amount of scientific research; they also create a political constituency who can be expected to make the case for the importance of continued (and if possible, increased) funding. Second, today the political process itself relies upon science to an unprecedented degree. Decisions about health care, environmental controversies, mineral resources, and national defense all depend upon input from the scientific community—whether to resolve debates, or allow decisions to be put off until more results are in.

There is still a great deal of resistance within the philosophic community to treating the epistemological and political aspects of science as two parts of a common phenomenon. What stands in the way of such a synoptic account? Like any discipline, philosophy has its presumptions. Traditionally, one of these presumptions is that philosophy properly begins in abstract theorizing distanced from personal needs, the hurly-burly of the marketplace, or the claims of politics. This distance (admittedly an unrealizable ideal, but striven for nonetheless) is supposed to deliver philosophical reflection from idiosyncratic personal influences, while guaranteeing objectivity and universality.

It has also led philosophers to pay scant attention to the examples they rely upon when they illustrate its theories. This oversight has gotten an increasing amount of attention in recent years. Much of Derrida's early work consisted in showing how often philosophy's central concepts consisted of blanched or "white" mythologies in which old metaphors became effaced through constant use.[7] A wide body of psychological and cognitive research has confirmed this analysis, demonstrating that thinking (scientific or otherwise) is fundamentally symbolic and analogical in nature.[8] Humans think in images: concepts are created through an analogical process, as we generalize from an example, having it stand as an image or symbol of a new case or of a larger truth.[9] There is nothing wrong with or even particularly limiting about our relying on images to understand the nature of things. It is simply the nature of human cognition. But we must be aware of the examples we rely upon.

Philosophers of science strive to provide a formal account of the nature of scientific reasoning. But in doing so, they have also illustrated their theories with a few notable examples taken from the history of science. These examples have overwhelmingly centered upon two places: the heavens and the laboratory. The stories of a few heroes—e.g., Copernicus and Newton, Lavoisier and Einstein—have served as models for the whole of the scientific enterprise. These examples have profoundly shaped our culture's conversation on the nature of science and the relationship of science to society's goals. In part, these choices simply reflect the historical importance of these figures—and the fact that most philosophers of science are trained in physics. But this fact reveals part of the problem—the lack of philosophers familiar with other fields, such as engineering and geology.

First, consider the heavens. It is a commonplace of intellectual history that Galileo and Newton shattered the medieval conception of the universe. Before their work, the cosmos was thought to consist of two regions: a terrestrial realm subject to change and imperfection, and a celestial realm that was the incorruptible and the home of the gods. Galileo and Newton demonstrated that terrestrial and celestial space were in fact homogeneous. The same laws of gravity governed both realms, and both were subject to the effects of time. The discovery that terrestrial and outer space were uniform meant that every position in the universe could be measured and calculated. A distinct realm of the divine was banished, as the laws of physics now situated and formulated everything.

But while in one sense Galileo and Newton destroyed the distinction between the terrestrial and celestial realms, in another sense they described a space for science that preserved many of the traditional features of the heavens. As Nancy Cartwright puts it, the laws of physics lie—in that they abstract from the unmanageable, deeply historical reality that we live within.[10] In their logical clarity, and in the view of science as distanced from our personal and political lives, the stories of Galileo and Newton offer an image of science with many of the traditional characteristics of medieval celestial space. After all, cannonballs of different weights *do* fall at different rates from the tower at Pisa: it is only by placing them in an idealized space (i.e., one without friction) that Galileo can identify a law that describes how they always hit the ground at the same moment. Similarly, Newton's laws of celestial mechanics offer a powerful image of scientific reasoning, but they also provide a convenient example of scientific certainty that is distanced from everyday affairs. Science viewed from the perspective of Newton's laws is disconnected from the traffic of everyday life, formulated in a rigorously mathematical way, and summed up in a few equations. Newton's research is an admirable example of the power of a certain kind of science. But how appropriate a model is it, given the types of challenges science must address today?

I am not suggesting that the only reason that Newton and Galileo are used (literally) as textbook examples of scientific advance is that their work fosters a certain image of science. But we must ask why these theories have the place they do in our accounts of science. Why, for instance, does nearly every college course in physics begin with Newtonian mechanics, rather than with an account of quantum mechanics, electricity, or optics? Newton's work is our paradigm of scientific knowledge: powerful, mechanistic, and certain (once we set aside the lifelike variables), and existing in an ideal, mathematical space. Newtonian mechanics thus fulfills both science's and society's dream of a scientific truth that does not entangle us in the complications of our social lives.

Of course, science did not stay in the heavens. But when the work of science was brought down to earth, it was located in a space that retained many of the characteristics of celestial space: the laboratory.

The laboratory is, by definition, an unreal space. Within it, conditions are parameterized, objects are constrained, and materials are purified. The space of the lab is utopian: in Greek, *ou-topos* means literally a "no place." The lab is a space abstracted from the rest of the world; it makes no difference whether a lab experiment is conducted in Dallas or Oslo.[11] And not only is the *space* of the lab idealized; in the laboratory, *time* is idealized as well. In the lab, history doesn't exist. Time exists, of course; it takes time to run an experiment. But the laboratory eliminates history—that is, the nonrepeatable and contingent flow of events, both natural and cultural, within which we live our lives. The defining characteristic of laboratory science is that the conditions and results can be repeated on demand.

The situation within the lab may be summarized as follows: what we gain in control, we lose in realism. The irony here is that while the lab sciences are considered the gold standard for scientific truth, the findings of the lab often don't apply realistically to the social controversies we face. The question that should lie at the center of the philosophy of (lab) science, but is too often treated as incidental, is "How do we relate the closed, ahistorical system of the lab to the open and historical world that we live in?"

This question has received scant attention from philosophers of science. And no wonder. For this question would force the philosophy of science to recognize how much the lab sciences depend upon analogical reasoning. Judging how the results from the lab's closed and controlled system relate to the open and historical world we inhabit demands skill at drawing apt analogies. Now, a great deal of work has been done on the role of analogy within scientific reasoning.[12] This work, however, has been concerned with the cognitive or psychological role of analogy in the creation of concepts—with how analogies help us imagine scientific problems—rather than with the analogical relation between lab and reality. And while the exact relation between lab and field is a vexed question, this much is clear: it will not be susceptible to mathematical formularization. Rather than in mathematics, analogical reasoning finds its home in disciplines such as philosophy, history, and literary studies.

Our reluctance to think through the lab sciences' fundamental dependence upon analogy with the field has given birth to two kinds of mischief. First, when society fails to apply laboratory results to the world in which we live, it encourages disillusionment with science. And second, it has sponsored the devaluation of other types of knowledge—in particular, the historical sciences and the nonquantifiable humanities—when they, by their very nature, fail to live up to the standards of the lab. The result of centering the philosophy of science on the two spaces of the heavens and the lab has been the creation of an enormously powerful intellectual apparatus with a very tenuous relation to social concerns. In this way, the philosophy of science has come to mirror the examples it has chosen.

II.

The fundamental problem with our discussions of science today is that we have separated the two elements of the discipline that must be held together. These two elements are the nature and status of scientific knowledge, and the relation of science to the rest of our lives. Separating these two questions has led to the development of a philosophy of science divorced from the concerns of policy makers and the public.

Consider a recent typical and popular textbook in the philosophy of science, Martin Curd's and Jan A. Cover's *Philosophy of Science: The Central Issues*—a 1,379-page volume published in 1998. Take a look at its table of contents:

Philosophy of Science: The Central Issues
Curd and Cover, eds., W.W. Norton, 1998

9 Sections, 49 articles

1. Science and Pseudoscience
2. Rationality, Objectivity, and Values in Science
3. The Duhem-Quine Thesis and Underdetermination
4. Induction, Prediction, and Evidence
5. Confirmation and Relevance: Bayesian Approaches
6. Models of Explanation
7. Laws of Nature
8. Intertheoretic Reduction
9. Empiricism and Scientific Realism

The first section of Curd's and Cover's volume is concerned with gatekeeping. The point of the articles in "Science and Pseudoscience" is to demarcate what does or does not count as science. By identifying what counts as a truly scientific procedure, Curd and Cover develop a criterion for demarking the territory of the philosophy of science: astronomy is in, astrology out; evolutionary biology is in, creation science out.

This is all well and good. However, Curd and Cover give much less attention to another type of gatekeeping—how we are to distinguish the realm of the *philosophy* of science from other areas of science study? The editors do not think this question deserves a section, or even an essay. Instead, they address it briefly in the book's introduction. There they argue that the domain of the philosophy of science is defined by such questions as "When is a theory confirmed by its predictions?" In contrast, Curd and Cover see the history and sociology of science asking questions such as "When was the planet Neptune discovered?" or "Why did Soviet biologists under Stalin reject Mendelian genetics?"

These distinctions are reasonable enough, but they also serve to obscure another set of questions that should be fundamental to the philosophy of science. In setting the philosophy of science off from the history and sociology of science, Curd and Cover frame the philosophy of science so that it focuses only on philosophical questions internal to the scientific process—the nature of the scientific method, what counts as theory confirmation, and the like. They have entirely set aside the other, larger task inherent to the philosophy of science—describing the relation between science and the other aspects of our lives. We cannot simply set aside questions of the relation between science and religion, science and art, science and language, science and politics, or science and technology as merely religious, artistic, political, and technological questions. Domain-crossing questions such as these are fundamentally philosophical in nature.

It is thus telling that we find no sections in the book on the relation between science and any of these domains. By what logic do they exclude these areas? Where is the section—or even an essay— on the role of analogy in science? Or, in a field that depends to a remarkable degree on a small selection of cases (Copernicus, Galileo, Newton, Maxwell, Einstein), where is the analysis of the power of examples? Or, given that half of all scientific research today is supported by public funds, where is the section that investigates the relation between science and politics? In sum, how has the philosophy of science come to be defined by an inward turn toward the lab and the epistemological procedures of the scientific method, rather than outward toward its connections with all the other domains of our lives?[13]

Defenders of the status quo within the philosophy of science have a ready reply. Such "externalist" concerns with how science hooks up with the rest of the world ignore a fundamental distinction—between the internal logic of the scientific enterprise, and its results or connections to the larger world. But this simply repeats the dogma of a philosophy of science based in the heavens or in the lab, where the world of science is essentially distinct from our personal and political lives. This distinction needs to be argued, not simply assumed, by books such as Curd's and Cover's, in an age when science has such a palpable effect on all our lives.

The defenders of the status quo have a second reply: "The field of Science, Technology, and Society was created to address those concerns." While the philosophy of science is properly limited to internalist epistemological questions (and a bit of gatekeeping), the field of STS was created to address concerns about the relation between science and society. But again, this begs the question. It assumes that epistemological questions intrinsic to science are unconnected to social, economic, and political issues.

These presumptions also highlight the dubious assumption under which the field of Science, Technology, and Society was created. STS chose to not contest the established domain of the philosophy of science. It left the internalist definition of the philosophy of science largely intact. It assumed that internalist epistemological questions were fundamentally separate from social-political questions. It is precisely this assumption that must be challenged today. For instance, it is clear that theory confirmation is not only a matter of epistemology. The standard for what counts as a confirmed theory also involves questions of time, money, personal and social commitments, and cultural values. It is relatively easy to demonstrate that what counts as reasonable confirmation varies according to a society's needs. For instance, in AIDS research, what counts as reasonable confirmation of the effectiveness or safety of a new vaccine may be set at a lower standard than in other, less pressing or deadly, cases.[14]

III.

Basing our image of science in the heavens and the lab has created a metaphorics of science as cerebral, ahistorical, and isolated from the other aspects of our lives. In contrast, a field-based philosophy of science offers us a more socially engaged and epistemologically realistic image of science. To see why, consider the distinctive nature of field science.

Science in the field proceeds at a different rhythm. Outside, in the open air, the scientist is subject to the elements. Rather than the controlled experience of the lab, the field scientist is immersed in a constantly changing sensorium that expresses the wonder and serendipity of experience. The conceptual and physical walls that isolated the lab scientist are gone; the field scientist passes through a shifting, frameless flow of events. In the lab, nature is constrained so that it will show itself in a regular fashion; in the field, the scientist must adjust herself to nature's patterns, cultivating a disposition of alert repose and anticipating the moment when the world reveals itself. The biologist may wait all day for the chance appearance of a species, and the geologist devotes hours searching for the telling fossil, splitting bedding planes in a shale unit.

While the lab narrows and controls the flow of information, the field's perceptual and conceptual kaleidoscope exceeds our capacities to sort, test, and categorize it. Field scientists develop intuitive skills for parsing knowledge in implicit, nonpropositional ways. Walk an outcrop with a seasoned field geologist. Years in the field have taught him how to sift through the superabundance of information and identify the significant anomaly—an odd dip in the strata, an unusual color along the bottom of a layer. Field scientists do not operate in objective geographical space conceptualized by Cartesian geometry. Rather, they move through a world of implied meaning constituted by the acting and perceiving body as it interacts with its environment.

In geological fieldwork, the black and white stripes of paired limestone and shale beds that are easily distinguishable at fifty meters grow indistinct at three meters, only to resolve themselves again at fifteen centimeters. Similarly, the land unfolds for the geologist as he passes over it, revealing an infinite number of perspectives that are integrated and contrasted in his mind. Of course, out of this, the geologist must abstract a testable hypothesis and numerical values. But these results are built upon the intuitive use of judgment in which the geologist selects—and constructs—a system of signs and blends multiple perspectives from a nearly infinite amount of potential data.

The field scientist's interaction with the Earth depends upon what Merleau-Ponty calls "motor-intentionality."[15] Motor-intentionality refers to the directed action-perception that operates before we consciously posit an object for examination. In driving a car, we do not consciously analyze traffic patterns and driving conditions. The experienced driver does not stare at the road, but rather scans the field of vision in search of clues: the faded yellow and white patches of the street lines, the paired flashes of animal eyes, the flicker of taillights, the telltale glimmer of bike metal. Like a surfer or a professional musician, the experienced driver is not so much following a set of logical procedures as moving along in a flowing river of experience, on the lookout for clues that point toward alternative futures. Indeed, while driving, it is dangerous to focus upon a single object, thereby losing the ambient awareness of one's surroundings. Experienced drivers do not experience a distinct separation between themselves and their automobiles. Such a separation only comes into play on a conceptually and linguistically objectifying level of consciousness. Similarly, fieldwork operates below the level of fully conscious intentional activity, which involves concepts and introspective reasoning, and above such mere reflex movements as the blinking of the eyes or the heartbeat.[16]

Of course, this intuitive awareness of the environment is itself the result of extensive training. Dreyfus and Dreyfus offer a phenomenological account of the stages in skill acquisition from novice to expert.[17] In learning to drive a car, the novice starts with conscious, rule-governed behavior: "Allow one car length between you and the next car for every ten miles per hour." Gradually such rules fade, replaced by immediate, intuitive responses to situations perceived in a holistic manner. In terms of our lived experience, the car becomes more and more an extension of our body rather than an object external to it. Field scientists—indeed, all scientists, and everyone who masters a craft—move through a similar set of stages. In the beginning, field scientists spend great amounts of time in the field consciously applying rules and guidelines. For the experienced fieldworker, however, the work proceeds smoothly and automatically, with little conscious reasoning.

These characteristics of field science provide us with an image of scientific reasoning that is much closer to the methods of everyday reasoning in our personal and political lives. Field experience presents inescapable spatial and temporal ambiguities; field scientists cannot subject their object of study to the controls of the lab. Nor can they duplicate the conditions they find a potentially infinite number of times. Rather, field scientists engage in a deeply human activity of interpretation, following out the logic of signs in which one infers relationships that are implicit rather than overt.

It is for precisely these reasons that field science has been neglected by the philosophy of science. The paucity and ambiguity of the data, and the nonrepeatability of the results, have been considered a weakness compared with the standards achievable by laboratory experiments. But this reaction should be stood on its head. By mastering such skills as working with an overabundance of ambiguous evidence within an essentially historical milieu, field scientists model powerfully the complexities of reasoning in science and in our personal and political lives.

The contrasts drawn here could be overstated; all of the skills identified with field science appear to one degree or another in the laboratory as well. But they appear most vividly within scientific fieldwork. It is also worth emphasizing that the distinction between lab and field science runs *through* as well as *between* the various sciences. Biology and geology both have significant laboratory components, while there is a field element to atmospheric chemistry. Since the subject of every scientific discipline is nature, even those fields most immersed in laboratory life must connect at some point with field experience. But we can still usefully distinguish between those disciplines that are more laboratory-based (e.g., physics, chemistry) and those whose work is much more closely tied to experience in the field (e.g., geology, ecology).

IV.

The days of being imprisoned within the messy, often unpleasant realities of life on planet Earth are almost at an end.

—John Casti, *Would-Be Worlds*

When considered at all, field science has been seen as a poor version of what properly occurs in the heavens or in the laboratory. But in fact, an understanding of science based in the nature of field-work adds a realistic element to our understanding of science, re-educating—and in some measure, reducing—society's excessive expectations concerning scientific knowledge.

Some will be dismayed at the suggestion that science should be allotted a more modest role in societal debates (say, in environmental questions, or in improving human health). Questioning science's status in society raises hackles—and not only in scientific circles. Many still hold to the view that scientific and technological progress are to be identified with progress *tout court*. Suggesting a more modest role for science in society is often seen as tantamount to repudiating the Enlightenment goal of progressively perfecting the human estate. But this is unfair. Calling for more appropriate uses of science in society does not make someone antiscience any more than promoting dieting constitutes an attack upon the food industry. Indeed, a more modest role for science even offers some benefits to the scientific community itself. For one of the greatest dangers to science today is that it promises more than it can deliver in terms of being able to resolve our political controversies.

But if fieldwork offers a powerful example of the science's nature, another image of science is coming to the fore, one that embraces and extends the philosophic assumptions underlying laboratory science. Today both the scientific community and society at large are turning to a fourth image of science: the computer screen or *cyberscience*.

The term cyberscience refers to claims that computer modeling presents us with a new paradigm for science in the twenty-first century. Computer simulations and models are being aggressively pursued across the physical and social sciences—from planetary physics to molecular genetics, from psychological metrics to economics and political science. But their greatest attraction is that they allow scientists to address precisely those areas that, up to now, have not been amenable to control in the laboratory. Computer models simulate phenomena that are too large, too complex, too expensive, or too historical to be placed within the lab: in a word, the phenomena studied by field science.

The rise of cyberscience has been supported by the steady expansion of computing power that allows us to manipulate amounts of data that would have overwhelmed earlier investigators—or crashed older computers. But the cachet of cyberscience also reflects the continued attraction of the Cartesian belief that reality is, at its core, something clear and distinct and amenable to mathematical formulation, rather than deeply sensual and interpretive in nature. Cyberscience speaks to the desire to escape the uncertainties and ambiguities of our lives. It establishes artificial worlds that we can control and manipulate— or for that matter, enter into via virtual reality. Cyberscience refurbishes the positivist dream of a type of knowledge that makes political debate superfluous. However, the question remains: How do these artificial worlds actually relate to the world that we live in?

The goal of a computer model is to fashion a set of equations that perfectly mimic natural processes. Once the model approximates reality, it can be manipulated in order to test out different scenarios. For instance, a climate model can be run by factoring in varying amounts of greenhouse gases in order to see how the results differ over time. But there is a hidden ambiguity here. For some of our most crucial questions, we either won't live long enough to verify the prediction (will global mean temperatures be 5° higher by 2100?), or we will do our best to never run the experiment at all (e.g., actually seeing what would happen if the hole in the ozone expands). As Naomi Oreskes notes, such computer "predictions" present us with a conundrum. Claims concerning the distinctive character of science turn on the testability of scientific claims. In these cases, however, we are equivocating on the terms "test" or "predict," when there will be no way to confirm the model in the time needed to make decisions.[18] One way researchers try to circumvent this problem is to run a computer model backward in order to retrodict what has already occurred: if the results match the historical data, the model is considered verified. But this assumes that the system being considered will function in the future as it has in the past.

Mathematical models consist of sets of differential equations that relate processes and quantities. These equations are of two types: those that model a system, and those that represent the initial and boundary conditions that put parameters around such a model. For example, in a global circulation model used to predict the possibility of climate change, there are sets of equations that describe basic physical processes such as the interaction of sunlight with matter and the natural properties of CO_2. These physical processes must then be placed within the context of our own particular situation—in this case, the temperatures, pressures, and geometry of the Earth.

Once a tractable analytic model has been formulated, the next step is to turn this model into an algorithm or sequence of steps that a computer can work with. There is an entire branch of mathematics—numerical analysis—devoted to working out the intricacies of this process. In many cases, simple numerical translations of differential equations are unusable, because the calculational steps lead to ever increasing errors, or instability. Numerical analysis has, however, developed schemes, or recipes, to deal with the subtleties of solving complex, interlinked sets of equations efficiently and accurately. A numerical model must then be translated into a language that a computer can understand (typically C or Fortran). At each of these steps, researchers are faced with choices of how to best represent the system that they hope to model.

A number of issues surround the use of these models to predict the future condition of the environment—issues that indicate that computer models, despite the suggestiveness, leave the scientific method where it has always been: in hermeneutics (e.g., data interpretation) and analogy (understanding how our results relate to the actual world we inhabit). As John Harte writes, models begin by postulating a "spherical cow," using simplifying assumptions in order to make the messiness of the real world more tractable to analysis.[19] For instance, in climate models, the Earth is divided into grids. Physical quantities within a grid box, such as pressure, temperature, and elevation, are averaged in order to present a finite number of quantities for computation. Furthermore, it is in the essence of a model that it will always abstract from, and thus falsify, the world that it models.

Not only do the computer models themselves depend upon a series of interpretive steps; the data relied upon to confirm the models is itself deeply hermeneutic in nature.[20] The point here—and the subject of the next chapter—is that the act of gathering data consists of interpreting sets of signs and traces of signs. Computer models thus face the same challenge that we found with laboratory results—how to analogize from closed and ahistorical systems to open and historical ones.

None of this means that computer models are worthless. In fact, they provide suggestive results for systems too complex to grasp intuitively. But rather than treating these new possibilities as a useful addition to the lab and the field, cyberscience has come to replace fieldwork. The presumption is that through computer modeling, the hermeneutically based field sciences can finally be transcended. Field sciences such as geology and ecology can be converted into "black box" disciplines in which the ambiguity and richness of field experience are replaced by the (purported) straightforwardness of numerical modeling. In the universities, programs in Earth sciences are closing. Field geologists are being replaced by analytic chemists and laboratory geochemists who conduct their investigations within the controlled environments of the lab and the screen.

The marginalizing of field science can reach startling heights. Federal funds have supported the creation of a program of virtual field trips whereby students can visit different locales via CD-ROM or the Web. In these programs students "visit" a hyperreal mountain stream. By moving and clicking their mouse, they place one of several virtual instruments into different parts of the stream. Such "field trips" are the apogee of laboratory control, the creation of a virtual world within which every parameter is controlled and instantly manipulated.

Without doubt, the digital revolution offers powerful new tools for scientific research. But our overdependence on these tools only serves to recapitulate the epistemological limitations of celestial and laboratory science. In fact, the seductive power of computers today makes appreciating the unique skills and perspectives of field science all the more crucial, if only as a counterweight to the excessive claims that are often made on behalf of cyberscience. The point is not that we should substitute the image of the field for the image of the lab. Replacing one image by another denies the complexity of our experience, scientific or otherwise. Rather, we should encourage recognition of all the images of science: sky, lab, field, and screen. Students, the scientific community, and the public at large will profit from the debate.

It is nonetheless worth emphasizing that science as it is practiced in the field not only offers the truest account of the epistemology of science; it also lies closest to the perceptual and conceptual processes of our personal and public lives. Other models of science purchase their greater certainty and predictability at the price of questionable applicability to our open, historical world. In a time when science is so powerful (for instance, in our growing ability to manipulate our own genetic material), it becomes crucial to understand the inherent difficulties when we move from the screen or the lab to the realities of our lives. As the case of Starlink shows, lab predictions concerning how things will behave in the field can go badly awry.[21] The field sciences offer us a more realistic account of the procedures, the power, and the limitations of science to address the controversies we face.

But how does the process of reasoning exemplified by the field sciences compare with the approaches relied upon within the humanities? Might not our culture suffer just as much from underestimating the powers of the humanities as it does from placing undue expectations on science to "answer" our problems? Could it be that the humanities embody approaches for making sense of those aspects of experience that escape or rebuff the scientific method? Or might the reasoning processes typical of the humanities already live (albeit in a cryptic form) within science?

In recent decades the humanities have slipped into a postmodernist scholasticism that is in many cases both irrelevant and supercilious. It sometimes seems that the chief contribution of the humanities to the cultural zeitgeist over the last thirty years has been to legitimize selfishness by supporting intellectual balkanization and ethical relativism. But the current dismal state of the humanities is also an effect of abandonment, as society has embraced science and technology as the agents of human progress. Despite turning our backs on this legacy, the slow accumulation of moral, metaphysical, aesthetic, and religious insights across the centuries constitutes humankind's chief repository of wisdom, as compared with mere knowledge. Humanists, rather than bemoaning the superficiality of our culture for not appreciating their research, should turn to the real work of demonstrating how their insights cast a bright light upon contemporary situations.

The next two chapters explore the humanistic aspects of geological reasoning. Through reconstruction and reconciliation across this intellectual divide between science and the humanities, we will be in a better position to use our intellectual resources in political debates about our environmental problems.

5

EARTH STORIES

More than two millennia ago the Greeks began their quest for *logos*—a pattern or rational order to the world. With Plato, Greek thinking came to focus upon a specific type of *logos*. Turning our attention away from our bodies, and from the body of the Earth, the Greeks directed the rational gaze upward, toward the stars, and inward, toward a pure mental order. Thus the Greek search for *logos* became a quest for a very particular type of order—one that was distant, regular, immutable, and certain.

The motivation behind this is clear. As Plato notes, our knowledge of things in the sensible world is always questionable. For how can we claim to truly know anything that is constantly changing? Time itself is the enemy of rationality, rendering every claim to truth inconclusive and suspect. Knowledge must be grounded in those realms beyond the corrosive effects of temporality. In fact, engraved in the portal to Plato's Academy was the statement, "Let no one deficient in geometry enter." Only in the realm of thought—and in the celestial sphere, a region considered beyond material corruption—could we find the conditions suitable for truth.

The creation of mathematics and geometry and the identification of the celestial order were watershed events in the progress of human rationality. With Plato defining reality as the rational, and rationality identified with the regular, immutable, and certain, the reality of the sensuous world was denigrated or even denied. Through its long history our culture has sided with this view. We have valorized the enduring over the transient—down to the present-day priority given to mathematics and the mathematically based sciences. Quantity and objectivity—the former understood as the deep essence of things, and the latter defining knowledge in terms of those things that we can turn into objects—remain the tokens of the real.

Embracing this notion of rationality has placed us in a peculiar situation. On the one hand, it has given us an unprecedented control over the world, resulting in the amelioration of suffering. Surely it is significant that we no longer lose half of our children to disease and malnutrition by the age of five. But on the other hand, this notion of rationality has deformed our personal and social relations. Issues of ethics, politics, metaphysics, aesthetics, and religion—those areas that cannot be parameterized and distanced, and which are immersed in time and contingency—are viewed as nonsensical. We hear a constant refrain: ethics is "all subjective"; politics "is only about power"; aesthetics is "just a matter of opinion." Metaphysics is dismissed as irrational nonsense, and religion has turned anti-intellectual (cf. the worldwide rise of fundamentalism).

Most to the point here, this conception of rationality, pursuing a perfect understanding of and perfect control over the world, has severely compromised the ecological order upon which life depends. The romanticism that long colored our view of non-Western and pretechnological cultures—seeing them as innocent, benign stewards of the land—has largely dissipated. Nevertheless, it remains clear that our scientific and technological culture has inaugurated a dangerous new epoch in our relation to the Earth.

The effects of this definition of *logos* upon geology—the discipline ostensibly concerned with understanding the Earth—are also clear. The limitations of what counts as "understanding the Earth" can be revealed, in part, by a comparison with medicine. What would we think of an "understanding of health" that wasn't concerned with actually making people healthy? For a normative or axiological element to knowledge is, or should be, as fundamental to the Earth sciences as it is to medicine. Moreover, these traditional presumptions about rationality have influenced not only how the Earth sciences are constituted but also their very origins. How does one explain the fact that while the study of the heavens has been pursued for over two millennia, the systematic study of the Earth is barely two hundred years old? It seems that our Platonic prejudices concerning the nature of knowledge have discouraged us from inquiring very deeply about the Earth. The Earth was "beneath" us— a subject too "earthy" to be worthy of serious attention. In contrast to the clarity of mathematics, or the mathematicized heavens, the Earth was inaccessible, impenetrable, and subject to sudden violence. And even before the discovery of geologic expanses of time, the vast expanse of the Earth, in both space and time, mocked the very idea of grasping it whole.

Except for a few early studies of mineralogy and metallurgy, the science of geology dates from Hutton's and Werner's investigations at the end of the eighteenth century.[1] We are only just now gaining an overall (if still incomplete) *logos* of the natural world (through plate tectonics and a basic understanding of the links between land, ice, ocean, air, and biota). But our greatest task still lies before us: integrating Earth-scientific knowledge and perspectives into our social, political, and spiritual lives. Grappling with the issues of global climate change, the loss of biodiversity, and the geologically imminent loss of natural resources—and for that matter, acid mine drainage—requires the marriage of the Earth sciences and the humanities. For it turns out that our limited understanding of rationality and our compromised relationship to the Earth are implicated. By humanizing both—bringing the tools and perspectives of the humanities to both areas—we will gain a better purchase upon our environmental challenges.

I.

Geology has received little attention from the humanities.[2] Certainly, contemporary philosophy has not recognized the field as a subject worthy of reflection. There is no philosophy of geology or of the Earth sciences as there are philosophies of physics and of biology. The two main schools of contemporary philosophy, the analytic and the continental, have ignored geology. It has been assumed (few even thought to argue the point) that examining the Earth sciences was unnecessary to understand the nature of science. Statements by philosophers on the status of geology sound a common refrain: "In conclusion, then, the Principle of Uniformity dissolves into the principle of simplicity that is not peculiar to geology but pervades all science and even daily life," and "Geology is a science just like other sciences, for example physics or chemistry."[3]

We can find a few exceptions to this general neglect. Ronald Giere ends *Explaining Science* by using the revolution in plate tectonics as a case study exemplifying his theory of science, and Naomi Oreskes et al. address the limits of hydrological modeling in a 1994 essay in *Science*.[4] Kristen Shrader-Frechette offers a book-length analysis of the assumptions underlying the storage of nuclear waste in *Burying Uncertainty*.[5] There are also two monographs that offer a philosophical account of the Earth sciences: David Kitts's from the perspective of analytic philosophy, and Engelhardt and Zimmerman's from a Continental perspective. Kitts's collection of essays—a geologist's spirited effort to create a theoretical structure for geology—never escapes the constraints of naïve analytic philosophy of science. Engelhardt and Zimmerman's book—combining the efforts of a geologist and a philosopher—in many ways anticipates the conclusions offered in this chapter from a fine-grained linguistic and semiotic level. Their book, however, focuses its attention upon questions of "communicative behavior" between Earth scientists, through an analysis of debates within scientific journals.[6]

Nothing shows this disregard of geology better than the lack of attention humanists have paid to the concept of geologic time. The discovery of deep, or geologic, time parallels in importance the widely acknowledged Copernican revolution in our conception of space.[7] The concept of time plays an especially prominent role within contemporary Continental or European philosophy. Nevertheless, philosophers and historians have ignored the Huttonian and Wernerian revolution's decisive role in reshaping our sense of time.[8] Strikingly, the typical conclusion drawn from the terrific span of geologic time is that it renders all our human efforts mean and insignificant. Geologic time opposes human time, rather than encloses it—mocking our efforts (see Shelley's *Ozymandias*)[9] rather than being seen as part of them and ennobling them.

Insofar as it has been considered at all, geology has been viewed as a derivative science, consisting of a few rules of thumb (e.g., the principles of uniformity and superposition) that guide the use of mathematics and the application of the laws of chemistry and physics to geologic phenomena. Geology, it was thought, suffers from a host of problems that undercut its claims to knowledge. These include incomplete geologic data, because of the gaps in and the poor resolution of the stratigraphic record; the lack of experimental control that is possible in the laboratory-based sciences; and the great spans of time required for geologic processes, making direct observation difficult, if not impossible.

The philosophy of science has viewed physics as the paradigmatic science. Physics was the first science to establish itself on a firm footing, and exemplified science's nature as certain, precise, and predictive knowledge of the world. Since the seventeenth century, all other sciences—and for that matter, the humanities as well—have been judged in terms of how well they live up to these standards.[10] Physics also fulfilled the requirement that scientific knowledge be analytically derived—reflecting the belief, originating with Descartes, that we understand objects and processes by breaking them down into their simplest parts.[11] A synthetic science such as geology could then be logically resolved into its constituents of physics and chemistry.

The geologic community itself has given the most attention to the philosophic aspects of geology. Gilbert's and Chamberlin's essays, dating from the classic era of nineteenth-century geology, embody the attitudes of natural history and natural philosophy.[12] In the twentieth century, various geologists have reflected upon the methodology underlying particular subfields of geology, and have offered general accounts of geological research.[13] Within the latter, the work of Stephen Jay Gould is especially notable, but the writings of Peter Ward, Niles Eldridge, and E. O. Wilson also show that the tradition of natural philosophy is not entirely extinct.[14]

While this work connecting geology with humanistic concerns has made real contributions to our understanding of geology and science in general, it has also been characterized by two qualities. First, it has accepted the description of geology as a derivative science. Earth scientists practice what Massey calls "the reverential reference"—treating physics as the paradigm of reasoning, trolling within physics or mathematics for an approach (relativity, quantum mechanics, fractals, complexity theory) that gives a patina of legitimization to their "softer" discipline.[15] (Whence the metaphorics of the hard and the soft? One may wonder, when scientists are praised for being "hardheaded," whether another region of being is the source of pride.) And second, for historical and cultural reasons that I will discuss below, philosophically inclined geologists have usually turned to only one of the two major traditions of contemporary philosophy—Anglo-American or analytic philosophy—for help with describing their science.

Are the Earth sciences best understood as merely applied and imprecise physics, vainly attempting to achieve the high degrees of resolution and predictability of physics? I offer a different view: geological reasoning consists of a combination of procedures that mirror the reasoning we use in our public and private lives. This combination of techniques is not unique to geology, but rather is present to one degree or another in most types of thinking, scientific or otherwise. But it is especially characteristic of the field-based Earth sciences. The sense of inferiority concerning geology's status as compared with other, "harder" sciences—its physics envy—is misplaced. A fully developed account of the Earth can provide the rational foundation for both our public and private lives.

II.

A prominent geologist describes the relationship between geology and philosophy thus: "Earth scientists do not find philosophical discussions of their field very interesting. In fact, many scientists treat the philosophy of science with 'exasperated contempt.'"[16] It is nonetheless true that the methodological self-understanding in the sciences, as well as our culture's understanding of the scientific method, is derived largely from the stories that philosophers have told. This description—science's self-understanding, and our culture's understanding of the nature of science—is significantly different from the account of science that has recently developed within contemporary philosophy and sociology of science. Busy with their own matters, most scientists and citizens are only faintly aware of this changed conception of scientific knowledge—or know of it only through the dust-up surrounding Sokal's hoax.[17]

To appreciate the nature of this new consensus, and what it means for our understanding of the science of geology, we need to first review the status quo. As mentioned, in the twentieth century, Western philosophy has consisted of two main schools of thought, analytic and Continental philosophy. The fundamental difference between these two approaches has turned on their attitude toward the nature and scope of scientific knowledge. At their most basic, the original claims of analytic philosophy (circa 1940) can be reduced to two: (1) all knowledge available to humans is derived through the method employed by science, and (2) the scientific method itself consists of an identifiable set of procedures sharply distinguished from other types of thought (other philosophic or literary approaches, such as traditional metaphysics, phenomenology, or literary criticism).

Early analytic philosophers such as Russell, Carnap, and Reichenbach developed a powerful characterization of the scientific method. Their conclusions may be summarized by the following three claims. First, the scientific method is objective. This means that the discovery of scientific truth can and must be separated from any personal, ethical/political, or metaphysical commitments. This is the basis of the celebrated fact/value distinction, which holds that the facts discovered by the scientist are quite distinct from whatever values he or she might hold. Personal or cultural values must not enter into the scientific reasoning process. Closely related is the insistence that we must distinguish between the logic of discovery and the logic of explanation. Identifying the particular social or psychological processes behind the scientist's insights is the job of the sociologist or psychologist. The philosopher of science is only interested in the logical procedures that justify a scientific claim.

Second, the scientific method is empirical. Science is built upon a rigorous distinction between observations (which again are understood, at least ideally, as being factual and unequivocal) and theory. Facts themselves are not theory-dependent; observation is commonly thought to be a matter of taking a good look at the world. The distinction between statements that describe and statements that evaluate is unproblematic.

Third, the scientific method constitutes an epistemological monism. Science has been viewed as consisting of a single, identifiable set of logical procedures applicable to all fields of study. This reduction of all knowledge to one kind of knowledge proceeds in two steps, those of scientism and reductionism. Scientism is the belief that the scientific method provides us with the only reliable way to know; reductionism further claims that it is possible to reduce all sciences to one science: physics.

It is important to note that this original research program of the philosophy of science, known as logical positivism, was challenged from within analytic philosophy by the early 1950s. Authors such as Quine, Goodman, and Popper raised fundamental questions concerning many of these points. But for our purposes, the crucial point is this: these debates stayed in-house. Analytic philosophy's basic orientation remained intact at least until the mid-1970s. Thus, while the exact status of scientific knowledge became more problematic, the general assumption that science (i.e., physics) was the model for knowing was not seriously questioned. Similarly, while the question of the objectivity of scientific knowledge may have been unclear, science was still thought of as essentially value-free when compared with ethical, political, or metaphysical issues. Finally, while the positivists abandoned their belief in the strict reducibility of all knowledge to physics, they still generally held to the existence of one uniform method for all the sciences.[18] Thus (and this point is worth emphasizing) while at the cutting-edge of analytic philosophy, the assumptions identified above were being questioned, the received wisdom—both within the philosophic community, and within the scientific community— retained a fundamentally positivistic orientation. Only with the Kuhnian revolution did this basic story concerning the nature of science come to be questioned.[19]

The claims of Continental philosophy concerning science can also be summarized in two points: (1) whereas science offers us a powerful tool for the discovery of truth, science is not the only, or even necessarily the best, way that humans come to know reality; and (2) the belief that there is one distinctive scientific method is a myth. Science has neither primacy in the discovery of truth, nor the unity and cohesiveness of one identifiable method, nor the distance from ethical, epistemological, and metaphysical commitments that analytic philosophy had claimed. Continental philosophy's basic orientation (since Hegel, circa 1806) had come from its attempt to define the scope and limits of scientific knowledge, as well as identifying the other ways we have for knowing reality. The two-hundred-year history of Continental philosophy can be seen as a series of attempts to invent or define other ways of accessing reality (e.g., dialectics, phenomenology, hermeneutics, existentialism).

In the nineteenth century, these two schools of philosophy engaged in a common debate on the nature of knowledge. But by the mid-twentieth century an informal division of labor had taken place. Analytic philosophy focused upon the intricacies of the philosophy of science. It viewed philosophy as ancillary to science, codifying and making explicit the logic of science that scientists already practiced, as well as deflating the claims of other, pseudoscientific and nonscientific modes of knowing. Continental philosophy ceded the analysis of science to analytic philosophy. Its main interest in science was not in scientific methodology per se, but in identifying what science left out in its one-dimensional approach to knowledge and experience. Continental philosophy focused on those types of experience not amenable to the scientific method: art, culture, subjectivity, and the force of the irrational in our lives. Continental philosophy insisted that the scientific method could not truly understand these areas.

Thus, as a first approximation, it is accurate to say that analytic philosophy became that part of philosophy concerned with the natural world. Continental philosophy concerned itself with those questions relating to our cultural and personal lives. One result of this division was that Continental philosophy (with its pluralist attitude toward the question of how we know) did not use its conceptual tools to describe the nature of reasoning in the various sciences, particularly the natural sciences. Another was that what most scientists and the culture at large came to know as the philosophy of science was derived from the tradition and assumptions of analytic philosophy, particularly in the form of logical positivism.

This division between analytic and Continental philosophy has only recently begun to change. The single most important cause of this shift has been the influence of Thomas Kuhn.[20] Trained as a physicist before turning to the history and philosophy of science, Kuhn shook the foundations of analytic philosophy of science. Kuhn undermined each of the assumptions described above, arguing persuasively that the history of science revealed that science proceeded in ways very much at variance with standard analytic accounts. Conceptual revolutions in science, rather than coming from a progressive elimination of errors, were often the result of abandoning one set of questions or assumptions for another set. Kuhn argued that there is often no common measure for comparing different accounts of a given set of phenomena; each account may be irreducible to any other, the differences in description resulting from the different types of questions asked, the different types of criteria used, and different research goals.

We can scarcely overemphasize the importance of this last claim, for it entails that knowledge, rather than being value-free, cannot be separated from human interests. Scientific truth depends as much on our perspectives and desires as upon an objective set of criteria.[21] For instance, the epistemological and pragmatic values attached to scientific research can find themselves in competition. If our criterion for understanding is predictive control, we may be willing to tolerate theoretical inconsistencies. If, on the other hand, our paramount goal is rationality, we may insist upon rigorous theoretical consistency. Moreover, societal perspectives also affect the process of research: defining the energy crisis as a problem of supply ("we need more oil") results in a different set of facts and a different range of possible solutions than if we define it as a problem of demand ("we need to conserve").

Kuhn made it possible to imagine a plurality of scientific approaches to a given problem, each with its own particular strength or virtue. The irony is that while Kuhn undercut the main body of assumptions of analytic philosophy, raising issues from a perspective more typical of Continental philosophy, he has been placed traditionally—if not always comfortably—within the framework of analytic philosophy. Conversely, Continental philosophy itself has spent little time examining scientific knowledge with the tools at its disposal.[22] But when we view the Earth sciences from the perspectives of Continental philosophy, certain features that had been left in the shadows begin to show themselves.

III.

Consider first the perspectives of hermeneutics, one of the most characteristic tools of nineteenth- and twentieth-century Continental philosophy. Hermeneutics is the art or science of interpreting texts. A text (by which is meant, typically, a literary work) is a system of signs the meaning of which is not apparent, but must be deciphered. This deciphering takes place when we assign differing types or degrees of significance to the various elements making up the text. The status of this deciphered meaning has been the source of some dispute: in the nineteenth century some claimed that, when properly applied to a text, hermeneutic technique resulted in knowledge as objective as that of the natural sciences. In the twentieth century, however, students of hermeneutic have claimed that the deciphering of meaning always involves the subtle interplay of what is "objectively" there in the text with what presuppositions and expectations the reader brings to the text. In effect, hermeneutics rejects the claim that facts can ever be completely independent of theory.[23]

Hermeneutics originated in the early nineteenth century as a means of reconciling contradictory statements in the Bible through a systematic interpretation of its various claims. In the early twentieth century, hermeneutics was applied to historical (including legal) documents to help discover the original meaning of the author. Theologians used (and still use) hermeneutics to argue which parts of the Bible to read literally and which metaphorically, and what weight to give to each part. Similarly, the literary scholar proceeds hermeneutically when she claims that a narrator's comments are to be taken seriously rather than ironically, as does the psychologist when he interprets a slip of the tongue to be significant or not.

In the twentieth century, however, hermeneutics has moved from being a rather straight-forward methodology of the *Geistwissenschaften* (i.e., the humanities; literally, the "spiritual sciences") to a more general account of knowing. Hermeneutic philosophers such as Heidegger have argued that *all* human understanding (including the natural sciences, although this was not his main concern) is fundamentally interpretive.[24] Not only books, but all of reality is a text to be read: rarely do we find completely objective data or information that is "purely given." How we perceive a thing is always shaped (though not completely determined; the world asserts its own independence) by how we conceive and act upon it with the sets of tools, concepts, expectations, and values that we bring to it.

Most of us are familiar with the hermeneutical aspect of understanding, the shift in our awareness of an object when we approach it with a fresh set of concepts or expectations. It is an experience that happens regularly to students when they are first introduced to a subject. Early in college, I found myself enrolled in an introductory art history course. Each class began with lights dimmed; the professor showed a slide of a famous work of art and gave us a few minutes to consider it on our own. Typically—especially at the beginning of the semester—I saw nothing of any significance in the art. Yet it became a truism that after a few minutes of lecture, the piece underwent the most striking transformation. Aided by the introduced concepts, the piece of art revealed itself for the first time. Like art history, with which it shares a strongly visual component, geology is a deeply hermeneutic science; the outcrop typically means nothing to the uninitiated until the geologist introduces concepts for seeing the rock.[25]

The claim that all human knowledge is fundamentally hermeneutic—that our perceptions are always to some degree structured by our conceptions—has portentous implications for our understanding of the nature of scientific knowledge, and for the relation between science and society at large. For it makes the question of human interests—personal, ethical and political, and metaphysical—intrinsic rather than extrinsic to the work of science. The theoretic assumptions that the scientist brings to his or her work—what counts as significant, and what research is worth doing—structure all that is examined, seen, and reported to one degree or another. Contemporary hermeneutics claims that this mix of percept and concept is fundamental to all human understanding. In the words of Merleau-Ponty, all understanding is a combination of eye and mind.[26] It is no longer viable to view the scientist as the purely objective reporter on reality. But this does not entail, except on the most radical reading, that all of our accounts of the world, scientific or otherwise, are entirely subjective. The truths of science, as with most things, fall somewhere in the middle.[27]

Hermeneutics does not pretend to offer methodological principles analogous to how analytic philosophy understood the scientific method. The role of hermeneutics is not to develop a set of rules for proper interpretation, but to clarify the general conditions under which understanding takes place. Nevertheless, there are three concepts that play a fundamental role in any hermeneutic process, including geological reasoning. These are the hermeneutic circle, the forestructures of understanding, and the historical nature of knowledge.[28]

The founding concept of hermeneutics is the hermeneutic circle. Heidegger argued that understanding is fundamentally circular: when we try to comprehend something, we understand the meaning of its parts from their relation to the whole, and conceive the whole from an understanding of its parts. So, for instance, the meaning of this sentence is understood in terms of the entire paragraph and chapter, and vice versa. Similarly, our understanding of a rock outcrop is based upon our understanding of the individual bedding layers within it, which are in turn made sense of in terms of their relation to the entire outcrop. This back-and-forth process operates on all levels; wholes at one level of analysis become parts at another. Thus our understanding of a region's geology is based on our interpretation of the individual outcrops in that region (and vice versa), and our interpretation of an individual bed within an outcrop is based upon our understanding of the sediments and structures that make up that bed.

Circular reasoning is viewed as a vice. But Heidegger argued that this type of circularity is not only unavoidable, but also the process through which understanding progresses. Understanding begins when we develop an intuition of the object's overall meaning. Without this initial conception, we would lack a criterion for judging the pertinence of a given piece of evidence. This provisional interpretation is called into question when details in the object or text don't jibe with our overall sense of things. This forces us to revise our interpretation of the whole as well as our interpretation of the other particulars. Comprehension deepens in this circular fashion, as we revise our conception of the whole by the new meaning suggested by the parts, and our understanding of the parts by our new understanding of the whole.

One consequence of the hermeneutic circle is that it puts to rest the claim that it is possible to approach an object in a neutral manner. Rather, we always come to our object of study with a set of prejudgments: an idea of what the problem is, what type of information we are looking for, and what will count as an answer. What keeps these prejudgments from slipping into dogmatism and prejudice— that is, what makes reasoning still possible, as distinguished from ideology—is the fact that they are not blind. We remain open to correction, allowing the text or object to instruct us and suggest new meanings and approaches.

Heidegger identified three types of prejudgments. First are our *pre-conceptions*, the ideas and theories that we rely upon when thinking about an object. Concepts are not neutral tools; rather, through them we get hold of an object in a specific way, opening up certain possibilities while closing off others. The terms "liberal" and "conservative" structure our political conversations, just as "ophiolite complexes" and "accretionary terranes" affect what we see in the field. These pre-conceptions include our initial definition of the object as well as the criteria used to identify the significant facts and the insignificant ones. Second is our *pre-sight,* our idea of our inquiry's presumed goal and our sense of what will qualify as an answer. Without at least a vague sense of what type of answer we are looking for, we would not recognize it when we found it. Third, we approach our object of study with a set of practices that Heidegger calls our *pre-having.* These are our culturally acquired sets of implements, skills, and institutions. In field geology, implements include the geologist's hammer, 0.10% HCl, a measuring tape, a hand lens, a Jacob's staff, pencil and paper, and a Brunton compass. In the lab, there is another set of tools: purified chemicals, mass spectrometers, computers, and a scanning electron microscope. In politics, we rely upon a third set of tools: fax machines, focus groups, opposition research, and mass mailings. Without a light microscope, one could hardly study the structure of nannoplankton; without daily polling, a candidate wouldn't be able to constantly reshape his message. With a different set of tools, we might gather new data that would give us a different (possibly quite different) sense of the world.

Heidegger's "pre-having" also includes the various skills that the scientist learns in the field or the laboratory: mapmaking, measuring strike and dip, preparing samples, cleaning and preserving specimens, and even wielding a hammer properly to split the rock without destroying possible fossils. Other skills would include the mathematical and statistical techniques used in research. Just as crucial, and often discounted, are the social and political structures of science: professors, graduate students, research groups, funding agencies, and professional associations. Science is a social as well as a mental activity; it depends on a community of scholars. Science proceeds through having colleagues to bounce ideas off of, professional societies and journals to define hot topics and favored lines of research, and graduate students to help run the labs and collect samples.[29]

A third point hermeneutics emphasizes is the historical nature of understanding. The claim here—distinct from the argument below—is that the particular prejudgments we start with have a lasting effect. Some may assume that, no matter what assumptions or goals we begin with, the scientific method will eventually bring us to the same final understanding of objective reality. Hermeneutics claims that our original goals and assumptions result in our discovering certain facts rather than others, which in turn lead to new avenues of research and sets of facts. Potentially important areas do not get pursued because of the lack of time and resources or the lack of sufficient commitment on the part of the scientific community, just as the history of past political choices structures the political landscape we occupy today. As decisions get multiplied over the decades, bodies of scientific and political knowledge come to have strongly historical components.

Heidegger's claims can be summarized in two theses. First, he rejects the view that data are purely given and that theories are totally objective constructions. Thinking always involves various types of values that are not merely unavoidable, but necessary. Second, science is not only something that one thinks; it is also something one *does*. Science is a social and historical activity, a *practice* as well as a set of theories.

IV.

Another feature of geologic reasoning is worth noting: its nature as a historical science. A historical science (a category which includes the disciplines of cosmology, geology, paleontology, anthropology, and human history) is defined by the role that historical explanation plays in its work. Explanations within the historical sciences involve the tools common to all sciences (e.g., the deductive-nomological model of explanation), but are also distinguished by three additional elements: the limited relevance of laboratory experiments, the problem of natural kinds, and the role of narrative.

As noted above, to the degree that scientific research is based on laboratory experimentation, it is essentially nonhistorical. In principle, the particularities of space and time play no role in the reasoning process. Not only is the space idealized, set up so that other researchers can re-create the experiment's conditions within their own laboratory, but in a fundamental sense history does not exist.[30] Of course, time and history are inescapable parts of every instance of scientific research: a chemical reaction takes time to complete, and every chemical reaction is historical in that it has some feature, no matter how insignificant, that distinguishes it from every other reaction. But our *interest* in chemical reactions lies not in chronicling the specific historical conditions affecting a given reaction, but rather in abstracting a general or ideal truth about a class of chemical reactions. A particular chemical reaction is approached as an instance of a general law or principle, rather than as a part of the great irretrievable sweep of historical events.

In the historical sciences, the specific causal circumstances surrounding the subject of investigation—what led up to it, and what issued from it—are the researcher's main concern. In geology, for instance, the goal is not primarily to identify general laws, but rather to chronicle the particular events that occurred at a given location (at an outcrop, for a region, or for that matter for the entire planet). Hypotheses are not testable in the way they are in the experimental sciences. Although the geologist may be able to duplicate the laboratory conditions of another's experiment (e.g., studying the nature of deformation through experiments with Playdoh), the relationship of these experiments to the realities of the Earth's history (e.g., the formation of the Rocky Mountains) will always remain uncertain.

The crucial point here is that the historical sciences are distinguished by a different set of criteria for *what counts as an explanation*. To borrow and adapt an example from David Hull, when we ask why someone has died, we are not satisfied with the appeal to the law of nature that all organisms die, true as that is. We are asking for an account of the particular circumstances surrounding that person's death. Similarly, in the Earth sciences we are largely interested in the specific histories of historical phenomena (a particular stream, a region such as the Western Interior Seaway, a trilobite species). We might identify general laws in geology that have explanatory power; but the weight of our interest lies elsewhere.

A second aspect of the historical sciences merits our attention. Historical entities present a unique challenge to the researcher; for how do we define our object of study? In some sciences, the objects appear as "natural kinds": for instance, the nucleus of an atom consists of neutrons and protons, a distinction well grounded in the atom's very structure. But historical entities do not spring into being fully formed, nor do they remain unchanged until their destruction. For instance, in investigating the history of the Colorado River (which seems to have run in different directions at different times in its history), we face the riddle of deciding when it first became "the Colorado River."[31] How close to the current Colorado River must it be before it qualifies? The researcher of historical entities—across the sciences and the humanities, and in our public or political lives—is faced with identifying the set of characteristics that define the particular individual, and with deciding how much change can occur before we have a new individual rather than simply a modification of the old.

Hayden White and David Hull argue that the concept of a *central subject* allows us to construct historical explanations.[32] A central subject is the organizational identity that ties together disparate facts and incidents. In human history, a wide variety of entities can function as central subjects: individuals or social groups, corporate entities (for instance, nations), even concepts (the idea of progress). In the Earth sciences there is a similar range of historical individuals: the Animas River, the Rocky Mountains, the species *Mytiloides mytiloides*, and the Pleistocene. Central subjects provide the coherence needed to construct an intelligible narrative out of a seemingly disconnected set of objects or events. But since these subjects are not natural kinds, they can be defined in different ways.

The question of central subjects plays an essential role in the debates surrounding acid mine drainage. Different parties presume different definitions of the streams in the San Juan mountains. Defining historical individuals like "Cement Creek" from temporal perspectives of 125 or 18,000 years ago can lead us to very different conclusions about our responsibility to clean up these streams. Viewing the issue in terms of the last 125 years naturally divides history into two periods, "mining impacts" and "pristine conditions." Framing it from the viewpoint of the last 18,000 years begins the discussion with the fact that *all* the streams were frozen and lifeless at the end of the last ice age. Indeed, from the perspective of 30 million years, the entire region was "polluted" by the mineralization that resulted from the area's volcanism.

Finally, the historical sciences are distinguished by the role that narrative plays in their accounts. In the experimental sciences, predictions are produced by combining general laws with a description of initial conditions. But the historical sciences are not primarily in the business of making predictions: rather than explaining an event by subsuming it under a generalization, they make sense of it by integrating the event into the flow of a story.[33] To make sense of a river, an outcrop, or a political event is to show how it is part of, and contributes to, a larger narrative. In science, narrative is commonly ignored: it is seen as a mere literary form lacking the logical rigor and evidential support necessary for real truth claims.[34] But this dismissal ignores the fact that narrative has its own distinctive logic. It also begs the question of whether scientific explanation itself depends upon the logic of the story.

Continental philosophers have been prominent in arguing that scientific explanation and narrative understanding in fact complement one another—science providing facts that parameterize an issue, narrative providing the overall goal and moral purpose of research. In *Time and Narrative* Paul Ricoeur claims that narrative—storytelling—is our most basic way of making sense of experience. In Ricoeur's view, scientific explanation itself depends on a framing narrative: defining the scientific project and making sense of its results depend upon the place that this project occupies within one or more story lines. These story lines (e.g., the pursuit of fame or riches, the righting of a public or private wrong, the desire for truth, or the wish for a better common future) provide the essential contexts for science. For instance, the development and testing of global circulation models (GCMs) gain their rationale in terms of our concerns with the ethical, political, and natural effects of future climate change. Earth-science information such as how much oil or copper we have left, how likely a catastrophic flood or volcanic eruption might be, and what the possible scenarios for our climate's future are makes sense only when it is placed within the structure of a story. Such Earth stories operate at different levels of generality: at their widest, these accounts frame not only our relationship to one another within a given locality, but also to the natural world itself.

Finally, narrative logic is distinguished from scientific knowledge by the fact that the former has an inherent moral structure. Narratives look to the future, not in the scientific sense of making predictions, but in Aristotle's sense of being concerned with final causes. A story always expresses a moral vision of what the future *should* look like (or in the case of dystopias, through warning us of an undesirable future). Historians, philosophers, and littérateurs excel at creating and interpreting the stories used to frame the work of the sciences, bridging the chasm that separates science and society.

V.

The Earth sciences only partially live up to the classic model of scientific reasoning. But rather than viewing itself as a lesser or derivative science, geological reasoning provides an outstanding model of another type of scientific reasoning based in the approaches of hermeneutics and the historical sciences. Geology is a preeminent example of a synthetic science, combining a variety of logical techniques to solve its problems. The geologist exemplifies Levi-Strauss's *bricoleur*, the thinker whose intellectual toolbox contains a variety of tools that he or she selects in accordance with the job at hand.

There are at least two reasons we should care about these claims. First, scientific reasoning in general and geological reasoning in particular are complex operations. It stands to reason that a greater degree of self-consciousness about the nature of the reasoning process can help the scientist to better evaluate the epistemological status of his or her work. Second, this argument points the way toward a more vibrant notion of reasoning within the sciences and our culture in general. Scientific reasoning is too often caricatured as a cookbook method that provides us with infallible answers. When the inevitable disappointment sets in, this misrepresentation damages both science and culture. The geologic reasoning process offers an account of reasoning more applicable to the uncertainties and complexities of our lives. We seldom possess all the data we would like for making a decision; and it is not always clear that the data are unbiased or objective. Therefore, we are forced to fill the gaps in our knowledge with interpretation and reasonable assumptions that we hope will be subsequently confirmed. The methods of a hermeneutic and historical science better mirror the complexities we face as historical beings.

We will soon turn to the social and political implications of these points of epistemology. But before doing so, there remains one other aspect to geologic reasoning we need to explore—the embodied and kinesthetic aspects of geology exemplified in geologic fieldwork.

6

THE PHILOSOPHY OF
(FIELD) SCIENCE

July 1993: First Exposure

Rock Canyon Anticline, on the bluffs of the Arkansas River. I stand on the edge of an escarpment that falls away to the west. It is stunningly hot. The stones beneath my feet clatter like broken china. Crickets buzz madly; the sun bleaches the bare cliffs to yellow, gray, and brown. Clouds roll off the distant mountains and stream over the land. The river is a muffled roar in the distance.

Searching for a break in the cliff, I find a route and descend—watching where I place my hands and feet, for rattlesnakes and scorpions are about—toward the valley floor below. Halfway down, I pause at a limestone ledge. With the back of my rock hammer I pry at a crack in a rock. Breaking the ledge, I see tiny red spider mites spill out across a mass of fossil clams. Traces of the dead are everywhere. The Earth is an ossuary; I am surrounded by bones. These cliffs are made up of the "hard parts" of creatures—fish and sharks, ammonites and clams and microscopic plankton—that lived and died 90 million years ago, when Colorado was covered by a vast sea that stretched from the Gulf of Mexico to the Arctic Ocean. Today's life, myself included, hangs on like lichen to a boulder.

Yet if this is an ossuary, it is an exceedingly strange one. While you can touch these rocks, it's more difficult to lay hands upon the world they hint of. Years ago, I wandered through a cemetery in Cambridge, Massachusetts. The gravestones dated from the 1600s, and most of the names had been effaced by wind and rain. Death so old took on a geologic tone: less tragic and more universal, leaving only the traces of ancient desire. These limestone cliffs are the bare-bones record of the struggle across time (GL:CH6).

95

To go into the field with a geologist is to witness a kind of alchemy, as stones are made to speak. Geologists reverse the work of Medusa, reclaiming worlds from the stone they're trapped within, drawing out a story from an adamantine palimpsest of lives and environments. But how do geologists perform this alchemy? What incantations are necessary to master the language of the Earth?

How does the geologist make sense of an outcrop? How does a mark or shape in a rock—or the very rock itself—come to signify, to be *seen as* something, indicating facts and relationships about its origin and history? Using my own experience as a case study, in what follows I trace the process of geologic interpretation by tracing the growth of my own understanding in the field. My case study will consist of a set of outcrops within the Rock Canyon Anticline in southern Colorado.

It is remarkable how philosophy has ignored the field sciences.[1] A search in the *Philosopher's Index*, the CD-ROM compendium of academic philosophy, turns up nothing on the subject of "field science" or "fieldwork."[2] And anthologies in the philosophy of science ignore the topic. A search of *Georef*, the equivalent bibliographic compendium within the Earth sciences, also turns up nothing. True, one does find in *Georef* a few listings of handbooks describing fieldwork techniques; and histories of geology sometimes touch upon the question of field methodology.[3] But these accounts are invariably empirical in nature, ignoring fieldwork's epistemological richness. If philosophic themes are broached at all, the account invariably relies upon stock accounts of how the results of fieldwork come from a steadfast allegiance to the facts. Geologic handbooks for the field present us with the anomaly of students being offered training in field science without any systematic accounting of fieldwork's epistemology—hermeneutic skills imparted, while being discussed in crude, positivist terms. Van-Brakel's comment concerning the philosophy of chemistry is even more applicable to the field sciences: "[T]he initial neglect of the philosophy of chemistry is due to the unanimous view in philosophy and philosophy of science that only physics is a 'proper' science. . . ."[4]

The standard answer to the question of how the geologist makes sense of an outcrop is that the geologist comprehends it by applying the principle of uniformitarianism. Uniformitarianism claims that the geologist proceeds by comparing observations made at an outcrop with a broad range of modern environments until a match is found. One finds, for instance, a likeness between the light and dark laminated layers of cores taken from the bottom of freshwater lakes, and outcrops of the wafer-thin layered rock in the 50-million-year-old Green River Formation in Wyoming.[5] From this, one can conclude that these outcrops represent an ancient environment similar to what is found in today's freshwater lakes.

This is an eminently reasonable approach, and one that surely advances our understanding of the story of the Earth. But the problem with this account is that it assumes that we will always be able to find a contemporary match—in other words, that the full range of past environments still exist today. But we are disabused of this assumption by a few elementary facts about the Earth's history. For instance, it is estimated that less than 10 percent of the Earth's past consists of times like today's "icehouse" conditions with permanent ice at the poles. Conversely, the "greenhouse" conditions typical of the past (times with high levels of carbon dioxide and of volcanism, and a much smaller difference in temperature from the equator to the poles) lie outside our experience.[6] Furthermore, some of the most typical environments of the geologic past (for instance, saltwater seas on continental landmasses such as the Western Interior Seaway, which covered a broad swath of land from Texas to the Arctic) no longer exist. Finally, even in places where we do find comparable modern environments, the scales of these environments are often quite different from those in the past. There is no desert today that matches, in age or extent, the tens of thousands of feet of sandstones found on the Colorado Plateau.

As an argument from analogy, then, uniformitarianism presents us with an enigma. The present is too small—and warped—a window into the past to provide the geologist with a full set of analogues. This is true in at least two senses. First, not only are we faced with the problem described above, of trying to draw an analogy from a nonexistent contemporary environment, but we also face a second problem: there are inescapable disanalogies between our human experience of time and the expanses of geologic time. The principle of uniformity can never tell us how to adjust modern conditions to rocks that have been altered by the slow effects of millions of years. Yes, we can travel to the Carolina Coast and excavate a cross-section in a beach, thereby uncovering burrowing insects and the trails they have left behind. But there is no process that we can observe today that will tell us how the insect burrow will look in a 100 million years. We can, of course, attempt to model these changes in the lab or on a computer, but this only recapitulates our problem, for we cannot be sure of the parameters we set, nor can we run our model for geologic magnitudes of space or lengths of time.

The point here is that what goes on at the outcrop involves something more than the mechanical matching of features between contemporary environments and strata representing the geologic past. Uniformity cannot tell us how to make our interpretation account for the differences between today's organisms and environments and those of the past. Thus, despite its usefulness within geology (and it must be emphasized that it *is* useful), there is a paradox in our use of uniformitarianism: it amounts to the assumption that time does not really matter. (This point is enshrined in the phrase familiar to geology students, "the present is the key to the past.") Uniformity is not wrong, but rather only partially answers the question of how the geologist makes sense of the outcrop.

What, then, are the other elements that constitute the geologist's work at the outcrop? My suggestion is that, in addition to uniformitarianism, geologic fieldwork depends upon a set of factors that includes the following:

• the development of a trained eye, whereby the geologist masters a set of templates that organize marks into a body of significant signs;

• the force of authority, as "old hand" geologists impart these templates to the student; and

• the cultivation of a distinctive mentality of alert receptivity.

This chapter develops these claims through the process of describing and imagining an outcrop. The goal here is to attend to the root nature of field reasoning, starting from the most basic questions imaginable, in order to reveal the processes through which one makes sense of our worldly experience. While this account focuses on *geologic* fieldwork, its conclusions should apply with modifications to other field sciences such as ecology, wildlife biology, oceanography, and anthropology.

April 1994: Describing the Outcrop

There is nothing so humbling as an outcrop.

—Pettijohn

Arriving early one morning at the Rock Canyon Anticline, at the Pueblo State Recreation Area, my thesis advisor stops the van in front of a hundred-foot-high escarpment. Handing me field notebook and a Brunton compass, he said, "See you this afternoon." I was to describe the local outcrops of the Bridge Creek Limestone, the first step in offering an interpretation of what this environment was like during the Cretaceous, 90 million years ago. I already knew a bit about the rocks, having visited this area before on field trips that offered an overview of southern Colorado's geology. These cliffs, I had learned, represented a "transgressive-regressive cycle." Over time, the shoreline of the Western Interior Seaway had advanced and retreated over this spot, depositing different types of rocks depending on where this place was in comparison with the shoreline to the west (website). I was also told that these cliffs recorded an extinction event known as the Cenomanian/Turonian Boundary. Somewhere in the rock face, one ecological community had passed into another—an indication that the region had undergone some type of environmental crisis (GL:CH6).

Today, however, I was left to my own resources. Where to begin? I was immediately faced with an arbitrary choice. Clearly it was impossible to survey the entire cliff face, which ran for several miles. But by what criterion would I choose one spot rather than another? An ash layer apparent at one spot on the cliff might disappear a few feet away, and spotting a slab of rock full of fossils could depend on the vagaries of how the rocks had eroded. Nonplussed, I merely headed for the cliff face that looked easiest to climb.

A novice in geology (with only courses in sedimentology, stratigraphy, and paleontology under my belt), I leaned on my philosophic training to guide me in describing the outcrop. Hermeneutics has developed various procedures for discovering or imposing order upon "texts." By approaching the outcrop in the same manner I would see if the basic interpretive strategies used in the humanities could work at the outcrop.

Three of these strategies are the search for contrasts, the discernment of patterns, and the recognition of aberrancies. For instance, when teaching Plato's *Republic*, one begins the task of making sense of the text by identifying basic contrasts between characters (Thrasymachus's role as a cynic, versus Polemarchus's portrayal as an innocent), and by detecting salient patterns (certain types of objections that are consistently raised by Glaucon rather than Adimantus). While this marks only the beginning of understanding, this approach helps to generate a template for grasping the text's basic nature. At the outcrop, it seemed reasonable to search for significant contrasts in color, shape, texture, and hardness. My quest for patterns became the attempt to find repetitions, either cyclical or progressive, in the rock layers.

The first impression presented by this cliff is its contrasting horizontal layers of black and white—a regularly spaced alternation between a dark, soft, and flaky rock and a white or cream-colored, more massive rock. As your eye moves up the outcrop, there is also a gradual thickening of the dark strata. The light strata are about a foot (30 cm) thick; the black units vary more, but are about twice as thick. The light-colored layers seem more resistant, and form small ledges that jut out above the dark rock.

But already I am stopped short by a riddle: this pattern is obvious only at a certain distance from the cliff, at a certain level of resolution and perspective. At ten feet, the division between the two rock types seems clear, but as I come closer the boundary between the two grows harder to identify. When I am flush against the outcrop, the very distinction between light and dark strata becomes questionable, as thin layers of lighter-colored rock now appear interwoven within the dark rock, and the dark rock itself seems composed of various layers.

What is the proper distance for viewing these rocks? While lacking an answer to this question, I assume that this impasse is simply a reflection of my lack of experience. Certainly a real geologist would know how to answer such an elementary problem. (Later, however, I discovered that the nineteenth-century art critic John Ruskin had discussed how artists might respond to this problem in their depiction of nature. In *Elements of Drawing*, Ruskin warns the artist against imposing a spurious clarity upon the world: to correctly depict nature, the artist must "have recourse to some confused mode of execution, capable of expressing the confusion of nature."[7] In at least some cases, the lack of clarity does not represent the observer's inadequacy; it is intrinsic to natural phenomena. Ruskin asks us to be wary of imposing a distinctness upon the world that it does not have. Similarly, in many cases there will be no ideal position from which to depict a scene, no perspective that trumps all other perspectives. Rather than waiting to be revealed in absolute clarity, nature reveals and conceals itself from every perspective and degree of resolution.) I climb down the cliff and retreat to a distance of several hundred feet. From this perspective the black and white alterations seem real, if indistinct. Simple description has become a tricky business. I climb back up, resolving to try to keep several perspectives (e.g., from close up, fifteen feet, and several hundred feet) in mind while describing the outcrop from a distance of only a few feet.

As for the rocks themselves, they consist of limestones (the light-colored areas) and shales (the dark beds). This is not so much a conclusion as simply a matter of definition: "limestone" is a sedimentary rock made up of calcium carbonate, which fizzes when you drip hydrochloric acid on it; "shale" is a fine-grained, finely laminated detrital rock made up of clay or silt. The limestone seems to be fairly uniform in character, massive and fine-grained ("micritic"), breaking conchoidally when I strike it with a hammer. The shale beds have more variation, seeming to divide into three types: a massive layer with some limestone in it, which holds a few egg-shaped concretions; a finely bedded layer that crumbles along thin layers ("fissile"); and an intermediate member that combines characteristics of the first two types.

I notice a number of gray or orange clay bands that widen from thin lines to a couple of inches in thickness. These layers appear either within the shale, or at the boundary between the limestone and the shale (often at the top of the limestone). Generally the bands that appear within the shales are thinner than those at the boundary between the two types of rock. There is no telling what I would have concluded about these layers on my own, for I come armed with a theory: I had been told that these bands are bentonites, the compressed and chemically altered ash of volcanic eruptions. As a consequence, description and interpretation of these layers are inextricably wedded. I could hardly see them as anything other than a bentonite, just as when we spot the inscribed marks "STOP," we see these runes as letters, and as a word with a definite meaning.

It was not until I returned to the outcrop with experienced field geologists that the importance of the third interpretive strategy, the search for aberrancies, became apparent. Experienced field geologists, rather than proceeding in the mechanical fashion that I had followed when looking for contrasts and patterns, first scanned the outcrop for features that "didn't look right": an unusual type of stain or structural feature, or an anomalously chewed up ("bioturbated") limestone. It wasn't so much that I had missed these features of the outcrop; they simply had not registered as expressing something particularly significant about the rocks. Scanning the rock for aberrancies, geologists quickly zero in on the outcrop's telling aspects—and are able to survey great stretches of outcrop in very short order. In fact, aberrancies often became the points around which geologists constructs an interpretation.

An "old hand" geologist working the outcrop exemplifies Aristotle's notion of *phronesis*, the judiciousness or practical wisdom that comes from spending years in the field. It is a skill that is visible in many areas of our lives. People new to a subject lack a sense of what constitutes the salient detail or revealing moment—whether the case is a political event, a scientific experiment, or a relationship in the office. Overcoming this deficiency has little to do with native intelligence, or following a set of logical procedures. Rather, it depends upon *knowing your way around* the topic, being oriented in conceptual space—or in the case of field science, in an actual geographic and geologic space. Bruce Foltz has described this type of knowledge as a type of reconnoitering. The most primary use of facts—scientific or otherwise—is to help us situate ourselves in the world, and understand the basic structure of the place we find ourselves in.[8] In addition to making it possible to exercise power over the world, knowledge helps us be at home in the world.

My lack of orientation in field science had another consequence; there was, in principle, an infinite amount of smaller-scale information at the outcrop that I could have described, but to go further in my description seemed pointless, even irrational. Lacking a criterion for what counted as a significant detail, to continue collecting and recording information would have been a random act. Without a sense of appropriateness for what constitutes potentially useful data, I lacked the basis for knowing what to describe and when to stop.

My account needed to address one other issue: the life in the rock.[9] I divided the fossils into two categories, macrofossils and microfossils—a distinction between the visible and the invisible. I saw fossils only in the limestone beds, with the number of fossils increasing as I climbed the cliff face. The traces consisted of bivalves (clams)—although there also appeared to be a few ammonite fragments. The character of the bivalves were indistinguishable from the bottom to the top of the cliff.

A few weeks later, I walked this outcrop with my thesis advisor. I noted that the bivalves were all of one species; he grabbed two fossils and was instantly able to demonstrate differences between the two genera of *Inoceramus* and *Mytiloides*. While I was not completely convinced (that would have required much more time in the field, looking at fossils squished in a variety of ways, getting better oriented to their various "looks"), it was immediately clear that I had looked past distinctive aspects of the different shells. Features such as the angle of the hinge line and the degree of curve in the shell's lineations announced clear differences between species. Experienced field workers are able to distinguish between different genera from the merest fragment of shell, picking out the significant feature in the midst of a cacophony of detail. The whole process is akin to working a jigsaw puzzle. When you first turn the pieces over, you are nonplussed by the task of distinguishing between such a monotonous blur of colors. But as the work proceeds, differences begin to reveal themselves: your eye catches the ever-so-slight shadings of red, suddenly recognizing them as the undulations of a velvet curtain. This experience also called into question my initial distinction between the visible and the invisible. I simply could not see what was clearly visible to more experienced geologists.

But what about the dark shale beds? During my time at the outcrop, I had collected samples from each shale bed to look for microfossils known as foraminifera. Back in the lab, I processed the rock from the bottom and top shale units by grinding the shale with a mortar and pestle, and then washing and straining the forams through a metal sieve. I then examined the resulting grit under a light microscope. I had only a passing familiarity with micropaleontology, and my only help came from another graduate student, who on a couple of occasions prompted me with questions as I looked through the microscope. But by prompting me to find salient differences, his questions at once affected my ability to notice distinctions.

And so I embarked upon a journey into a world distant in both space and time, scrutinizing the shells ("tests") of creatures of infinitesimal size and nearly a hundred million years old. They were strange geometric beasts: in the bottom shale bed they came coiled, cone-shaped, and globular, sometimes symmetrically arranged around a single axis, sometimes seeming randomly stuck together spheres. In the upper bed, I also found the globular shapes (both arranged around and without an axis) and those shaped like a cone, but this bed also revealed two new types: a coiled, cocoon-shaped creature and a columnar, ribbed, rectangular beast. Lacking any larger interpretive framework in which to put these discoveries— and not wanting at this stage of my work to give myself over to the paleontological literature, which would have rigorously defined all of these specimens—I put them aside, and they played no further role in my description or interpretation of the outcrop (GL:CH6).

Finally, I looked for the influence of large-scaled features (e.g., faults, igneous intrusions, evidence of metamorphism) upon the outcrop. The layers themselves were close to horizontal, with little sign that the rocks had been deformed after deposition. It seemed that the Arkansas River had simply cut down through a section of Cretaceous-age strata. (It was later pointed out to me that this exposure of rocks was dependent upon a regional uplift—the "Rock

Canyon Anticline"—and that this dome was quite apparent to the trained eye. It was there to be seen, and a trained geologist would be on the lookout for just such a feature to explain the geomorphology of the area.)

May–July, 1994: Imagining the Outcrop

> The universe is perfused with signs, if it is not composed exclusively of signs.
>
> —Peirce (1955)

By mid-May, I had made several more visits to the outcrop. I spent these days peering at the rock, taking notes and making sketches, cracking stones for fossils, musing and imagining. The visits were separated by a few weeks, and complemented by journeys to other localities for comparison. I also read a great deal in the literature on the late Cretaceous Western Interior Seaway (GL:CH6). The massive amount of material on this obscure subject is a telling commentary on the state of knowledge production today. My own research became interwoven with and dependent upon a community of researchers—a community effort to understand the goings-on in the middle of the North American continent 90 million years ago.

Learning the language of the outcrop required time to mull things over as new questions or insights slowly formed. With each of my visits the rock became more articulate. Formerly meaningless marks gained significance as I learned to fit them within—or found that they contradicted—a narrative of the region. I, of course, endeavored to test my ideas against the facts at hand, but the sources of these ideas were literally daydreams, as I imagined the processes that might have given birth to what now lay before me: the slow rain of calcium carbonate particles onto the floor of an ocean, or lazy rivers from nearby highlands delivering clay-size fragments into the depths.

But when I first wrote up an account of the outcrop at Rock Canyon, I did not mention these musings. Instead of reveries, I focused upon proof. I concentrated not on what I thought had actually happened, but on those aspects of my account that I could demonstrate. Intimidated by an imagined audience—skeptical geologists—I concentrated on replying to questions such as "But can you prove that? How do you know it's the case?" I thus spent a great deal of time working out a succession of inferences and deductions based on what I had found at the outcrop. My goal was to strictly follow out the logic of the outcrop, establishing points in a linear fashion, taking the reader from the first, most obvious point onward. So, for instance, I traced out the logic that would allow me to claim that this region now nearly a mile above sea level had once been beneath the sea:

1. The rocks before me were sedimentary in origin. In the dark rock I could see bedding, and although the white rock was massive rather than layered, the presence of fossils testified to its sedimentary origin.

2. These sediments had been deposited in an aqueous environment. A web of inference, no single piece of which was decisive, but the total weight of which was convincing, supported this claim: (a) Most preserved sedimentary environments are of subaqueous origin. (b) Those that are not have distinctive geometries (e.g., alluvial fans) or sedimentary structures (eolian crossbedding, graded bedding, mudcracks), which the rocks of the Bridge Creek Formation lack. The rocks of the Bridge Creek suggest a low-energy, uniform depositional environment across space and time. And (c), there are subaquatic fossils (bivalves and foraminifera) in the outcrop.

3. That these are marine (rather than freshwater) rocks is suggested by the following: (a) the regional extent of these rocks (itself a fact accepted largely on the authority of others); and (b) again, the presence of bivalves and foraminifera (although freshwater bivalves and forams do rarely occur). All of this implies that this region was part of an ocean or inland sea that once covered what is now Colorado, and more generally the High Plains and Intermountain West.

But I eventually realized that this approach missed the point. Not the least reason was my difficulty in distinguishing between the conclusions I had come to based on what I had actually seen at the outcrop, versus those I had acquired through the authority of others (from books or articles, or the classes or random comments of geologists). More centrally, however, it became clear that this approach proved peripheral to the central goal of my project: offering a description of the growth of geologic insight. One cannot set aside the question of proof when discussing the matter of geologic vision, for one must be able to distinguish between reality and the phantasms of one's imagination. Nevertheless, geologic seeing does not in the first instance consist of a series of deductions and inferences from a set of data. Rather, a geologist is someone who has learned the language of the Earth.

As "language" is customarily understood, this claim must be treated as merely a play on words. Language, it is said, consists of a series of arbitrary signs designating objects or events. Language is the possession of the human community, or at most a few animal species, who *intend* to communicate a meaning. The phrase "language of the Earth" cannot be taken seriously. Lacking consciousness, rocks cannot intend to signify.

But is it possible to signify a meaning without intending to? A criminal who leaves clues to his identity does not intend to tip off the detective, nor does an animal mean to leave tracks leading to its den. In fact, every existing thing leaves traces of its history and condition. To see the semiotic (meaning-laden) nature of reality, consider the account of the nineteenth-century American philosopher Charles Sanders Peirce.[10] Peirce distinguished three types of signs. Icons are based in actual resemblance: for instance, a portrait. Indices are cases in which one postulates a natural or causal link between the mark and the object it is taken as indicating. This is the realm of natural signs, which may be as prosaic as the piled branches left from a past flood along a riverbank, or as esoteric as oxygen isotope data used for determining temperature regimes in the Cretaceous. Third, there are cultural signs, where the relation between the signifier (i.e. the word, the phonic or written sound) and the signified (the concept signified) is arbitrary, a matter of convention. Defined in this way, we can see everything that exists as a series of marks that bear a meaning by referencing the larger world enclosing them. It is this idea that Peirce had in mind when he claimed that "the universe is perfused with signs, if it is not composed exclusively of signs."

Semiotics is the discipline dedicated to developing a general theory of signs. While semiotics has been developing for over a century, its almost exclusive concern has been with the character of cultural (i.e., literary) signs, those signs that are true by convention. Thus "dog" in English (or *Hund* in German) arbitrarily links a set of sounds with the idea of Fido. Semiotics has largely overlooked the study of natural signs, signs that are true not by convention but by virtue of natural, i.e., causal relations (e.g., a cumulo-nimbus cloud as a sign of an impending thunderstorm). One of the foremost students of semiotics has remarked upon "the utter, frightening innocence of most practitioners of semiotics about the natural order in which they and it are embedded."[11]

By Peirce's reckoning, any mark or presence is a sign—once someone has mastered the language of a given domain of experience. But while anything *can* function as sign, it is too much to suggest that the world is "composed exclusively of signs." Albert Borgmann notes, "If the world consisted of signs only, nothing would be present and address us in its own right."[12] We see, for example, the signs of maturity in a child, and may even see her as a sign of things to come. In the same way, the jonquils outside my window are a sign of spring for both the bees and me. But both the child and the flowers also stand outside the economy of signs, standing forth in the vibrancy of their reality.

Geologists learn the grammar and logic of stone. The geologist gleans signs—what the detective calls clues, the gambler tells, and the physician symptoms—traces that indicate or point toward something absent (in the case of the criminal, or the geologic past) or inaccessible (in the case of a disease, or the interior of the Earth). These marks acquire a meaning by hooking up and referring to a network of relations—the mark's context or background. For the geologist, a trace in a rock gains meaning by being seen *as* something, part of a larger story, such as when a burrow mark is seen to indicate facts about the depth of the water and the age of the rock.

The geologists who accompanied me seemed to detect a potential meaning in nearly every mark and shape in the rock. Of course, these were merely potential meanings, surmises that had to be verified. But while the process of testing and verification is commonly viewed as the central activity of science, this verification depends upon the prior act of imagining potential meanings. Without first imagining the mark or shape as a sign, a scientist would have nothing to try to demonstrate.

My time at the outcrop also diverged from that of geologists in the way I treated signs. Novice students of literature, struggling to reveal the meanings of a text, will often search for a one-to-one correspondence between an image and a meaning. They view a poem simply as a code to be deciphered. Similarly, early on, I relied on the simplistic application of stratigraphic principles, reasoning clumsily that "shale means shallower water and closer to shore, and limestone deeper water and farther from shore; thus the beds before me represent cycles of transgression and regression." I found, however, that there were a number of other explanations: water depth and distance from shore can remain the same, while the relative

amount of sediment input varies by factors such as changes in climate. I needed to look at the outcrop as a language—a system of in-
terrelating and counterbalancing processes, tectonic and climatic
activity, Milankovitch cycles, changes of sediment production and
productivity.

August 1994: The Lodge at Starved Rock, Illinois

Chris and Teri, and De and I, were spending a few days together
in northern Illinois. We had been friends since undergraduate days.
Chris had just finished a Ph.D. in literature on Joseph Conrad.

Chris and I pass outside through the main entrance. I glance
down at the roughhewn flagstones forming the walkway.

"Hey—fossils."

"What? Where?" Chris pauses, but is skeptical.

"Look at these flagstones."

". . . Nah, that isn't anything. Let's go." He heads for the car.

"C'mon back. Take another look."

He leans over the rock for a moment. "Those are just patterns in
the rock."

"They're patterns, all right, but they're also signs. Think
of them as circumstantial evidence—of a crime committed a couple
of hundred million years ago. Take a few moments to stare and
imagine."

He puts his face close to the rock and is silent for a time. "How
can you be sure that it's a fossil?"

"Who's sure? Were you sure that it was a raccoon that we saw
last night? But consider, do these lines look random? See how it's
patterned, having the organized look of something organic? The elegant curve from tip to tip?"

"That's all the proof you got?"

"People have been thrown in prison on less . . . really, the point
is that you have to change your frame of reference. Geologists are
detectives. They read clues. They pick up on telltale traces and piece
them together into a convincing story. Given enough time, we could
put together a fair amount of supporting evidence here . . ."

Two grown men on their hands and knees at the doorway to a
lodge attract attention. A stranger pauses, and asks, "What'cha
doing?"

"Take a look," Chris says. "These are fossils in these rocks."

"What? . . . Nah."

"No, really—see these curved lines? It's some kind of creature."
The man peers at the stone for a moment. "That's no fossil."

"But you can't see it from there: come down and take a closer look." The man bends over, staring at the stone for a moment longer, then starts to edge away.

"That's no fossil. There aren't any fossils around here."

August 1995: Some Conclusions

> What we call a visible is . . . a quality pregnant with a texture, the surface of a depth, a cross section of a massive being. . . .
>
> —Merleau-Ponty, *The Visible and the Invisible*

Throughout its history, philosophy's predominant concern has been with *logos*. *Logos*, a Greek word meaning "word" or "order," names the attempt to make sense of experience, to put things together as a coherent whole. Philosophy, and later science, has focused on describing the various types of order found in the world. This sense of logic is still with us, appearing in terms such as biology or psychology, which denote the systematic arrangement of miscellaneous facts into ordered bodies of knowledge. It is also the origin of today's more common usage, which correctly but narrowly understands logic as referring to a set of operations that govern valid or reliable inference.

But what about the logic of vision, the process by which the geologist puts together a narrative of the outcrop? My time at the outcrop argues that uncovering the *logos* of an outcrop is not a rote procedure, but instead depends upon a complex mental, visual, and kinetic process. The trained geologist does not merely stare at the outcrop and collect data like one picks up acorns. He has learned to see the mark or shape as representing a complex set of interactive processes captured in stone.

Vision is often imagined as a simple receptivity; seeing is just a matter of taking a good look. But rather than merely receiving information, the eye acquires its own education. There is a simultaneous obscurity and superabundance of data that the simple application of uniformitarian principles cannot organize. Rather, the eye and mind interact to make data coherent. Insight comes through the receptive eye that *dreams* the outcrop.

Much of my education in field science has come through reflecting on my own failures in seeing what was obviously there. But my chagrin at missing the obvious has been lessened by reports of geologists who have suffered the same failure. In his autobiography, Charles Darwin recalls going into the field in Wales in 1831 with Adam Segwick, nearly a decade before Louis Agassiz's theory of continental glaciation:

> Neither of us saw a trace of the wonderful glacial phenomena all around us; we did not notice the plainly scored rocks, the perched boulders, the lateral and terminal moraines. Yet, these phenomena are so conspicuous that . . . a house burned down by fire did not tell its story more plainly than did this valley.[13]

But while this experience is ubiquitous among geologists, the process by which one moves from blindness to insight has been little analyzed by either science or the philosophy of science. Nonetheless, this experience is present throughout science—as well as in reading a poem and in judging the intonations and body language of a salesman. The act of semiosis—learning to see something as a sign expressing meaning—is arguably humanity's most basic rational activity. It is *this* skill, rather than propositional and predicate calculus, that should be taught in logic classes; indeed, it should find a home in every discipline across the curriculum. Skill in semiosis is found in the scientist's work in the lab or the field, the physician's ability to recognize signs of incipient illness, and our ability to read the motivations of the people we meet.

The skills exemplified in geologic fieldwork may be placed under two headings: thinking in the interrogative mood, and the visible and the invisible.[14] To see the former, turn again to Plato's *Republic*, a dialogue concerned with the question "What is justice?" One can read the text many times before asking, Why does the story begin with Socrates' friends grabbing him by the sleeve and playfully forcing him to stay for the afternoon?[15] It is unlikely that most readers actually conclude that the incident is insignificant. It is more likely that readers never raise the question at all, assuming that it is only a bit of stage setting before the real dialogue begins. But once the question is posed, this innocent beginning takes on a meaning that influences one's interpretation of the entire work. For this small act of mock antagonism broaches the issue of the relation between violence and reason. Does the threat of violence itself motivate us to be reasonable? Is reason itself a type of violence, as when we speak of the "force of an argument"? And so on. The meaning of any text—be it an outcrop, or a political event—does not simply lie on its surface. If the world is to give up its secrets, one must habitually pose questions.

The geologist doesn't simply record data that falls upon the eye, but rather learns a certain style of interrogative thinking. The question, "Does the Bridge Creek Formation begin with the bottom-most limestone bed?" is not terribly complex, but for a long time no one thought to ask it. The formation below the Bridge Creek (the Hartland) consists of tens of feet of gray shale, and so it is natural for one to think that the Bridge Creek Formation begins with the first appearance of limestone. But Don Eicher thought to pose this question, and found that the fossils in the Hartland divided this seemingly uniform shale into two different units: the upper half meter of what appeared to be the Hartland Shale had foraminifera matching the shale units of the Bridge Creek.[16] The region's environmental history was reinterpreted as a consequence of Eicher's thinking in the interrogative mood.

Like vision itself, visual intelligence depends upon background awareness. Vision is not structured in the subject-verb-object terms of our language. The logic or structure of an image is a "figure-background" relation; a point of focus is surrounded by a penumbra of generalized awareness. Of course, we can shift our point of focus to a place that previously was background. But we cannot focus upon the background as such. This ambient awareness of one's surroundings involves another, more subtle and intuitive type of *logos*—an orienteering type of knowledge in which we come to know our way around a subject. Knowing your way around the Grand Canyon—or New York City—does not mean that you are familiar with its every nook and cranny. But it does imply that you are oriented in that space, and that if you were dropped into an unfamiliar side canyon, you would know where to look for water or where to find a break in the cliffs to climb out.

It is possible to understand the basic meaning of a term, or adequately manipulate a set of symbols, without having a rich, holistic sense of how a point properly plays out in practice. One can know the rules of a game without being good at playing it, or know basic stratigraphic principles without being able to properly apply them to a particular outcrop. In the midst of a game, an athlete cannot explicitly conceptualize the flow of information coming in from all directions. The situation is too complex, and the data received are too obscure (e.g., by the roar of the crowd, or a pair of hands in the face).

But amidst this confusion, the athlete is still able to perfectly place a pass.

Visual intelligence also involves more than the use of our eyes. Spatial understanding is kinetic; to understand three-dimensional space, one must move through it. Geology involves a tactile and kinesthetic type of reasoning, demanding an active and mobile body rather than the disembodied intelligence of mathematical knowledge. I needed to walk—and climb—the cliffs in order to understand them, to see them from a variety of angles and perspectives. The geologist stares at the outcrop, of course. But she also moves around in order to see it at different angles. She strikes or digs the rock out, feeling its density and resistance. She directs her body back and forth, left and right, to take in the different geological features, intuitively seeking an optimum distance and observational angle for the features being considered. When we view an object, we seek "a direction viewed from which it vouchsafes most of itself." Merleau-Ponty calls this the tendency toward gaining a "maximum grip" upon the environment.[17] In some cases, however—for instance, in viewing the alternating layers of limestone and shale in the Bridge Creek Formation—there is no single point of maximum grip. We must try to hold onto a series of irreconcilable views of an object— geologic fieldwork as cubism.

To see the relation between the visible and the invisible, consider the work of the nineteenth-century French painter Paul Cézanne, especially his repeated rendering of Mont Sainte-Victoire near Aix-en-Provence (GL:CH6). Cézanne dismissed the title of "impressionist." He described his goal as painting how we actually see the world, the lived perception of an object rather than a geometric or photographic one. He remarked to his friend Bernard, "[W]e must develop an optics, by which I mean a logical vision—that is, one with no element of the absurd." Cézanne's wife described his manner of working: "He would start by discovering the geological foundations of the landscape, convinced that these abstract relationships, expressed, however, in terms of the visible world, should affect the act of painting."[18] For Cézanne, the surface of an object is not simply a two-dimensional flat plane, but rather the surface obscuring a hidden depth, which reaches its expression at the surface.

Cézanne's goal was a rigorous fidelity to the object. But instead of pursuing this by drawing the outlines of things and then coloring them in, Cézanne constructed objects not by lines but by color. "The contour of an object conceived as a line encircling the object belongs not to the world but to geometry . . . the world is a mass without gaps, a system of colors across which the receding perspective, the outlines, angles, and curves are inscribed like lines of force. . . ."[19] An object's shape is constructed from the inside out; the object's edge is an ideal limit rather than a line, depicted through a series of receding contours. "Nature," Cézanne urged, "must be seen from the inside."

A vivid description, to be sure. But how does Cézanne's description of how he approached painting relate to the geologist's work at the outcrop? And Cézanne's phrase—that "nature must be seen from the inside"—what could this mean? Far from being merely an impressionist's reverie, Cézanne offers us a nuanced account of the geologist's actual experience and procedure in the field. Rather than simply collecting data, the geologist *envisions* the outcrop, struggling to see it as a system of colors or of shapes, but in any case as a system that evolves into a template or *logos* that the facts will fit within and modify. The geologist eventually converts this initial experience into the languages of mathematics and geometry, making it both precise and verifiable. But the essential act here is the act of envisioning.

In his working notes to *The Visible and the Invisible*, Merleau-Ponty explores how what we do not see guides, relates to, or interacts with what we do see. In vision, there is a relation between the surface of things and the depths hidden to us. In sketching a face, the artist tries to express the "the surface of a depth"—the inner nature of the individual that finds its expression at the surface. In a similar fashion, the geologist gives us "a cross section of a massive being," interpreting the two-dimensional surface as an expression of a three-dimensional structure. Walking Six Mile Fold in Colorado with a structural geologist, I struggled to see a two-dimensional surface in terms of the underlying relationships. What was objectively there was a sinuous limestone bed outcropping across the surface of a ridge. But once I saw it from the inside, this became a fold bisected by a stream. In like manner, the geologist sees *into* the rock: translating two dimensions into three; grasping the nature of an object or pattern by mentally rotating, unfolding, or completing it in space; relying upon his knowledge of the outcrop's geochemistry to inform an interpretation; or evaluating the present outcrop in terms of others across a region. In all of these cases, the geologist's vision is structured or guided by what is not visible. The practiced geologic eye has learned how to penetrate the object—probing it, testing it, sizing it up—seeing the surface as a surface of a depth, rather than simply as a surface.

How, then, does the geologist makes sense of the outcrop? One aspect surely follows what is taught in introductory historical geology: through applying uniformitarian principles. Seeing the outcrop is in part a logical process that depends upon syllogisms no different from "All men are mortal; Socrates is a man; therefore; Socrates is a mortal." In stratigraphy, the syllogism might be: "The coarseness of sediment is a measure of the stream's transporting power; sediment becomes more fine-grained from east to west across the section; therefore, the transporting power of the stream has lessened as we move toward the west." But logic isn't simply, or even primarily, a mechanical process grinding out such statements. Logic in the sense of *logos* identifies that overall structure or context within which things take on significance. The first sense of logic can be taught in a rote way. But logic in the second, more fundamental sense relies upon *knowing your way around* the outcrop, learning to pose appropriate questions, and *envisioning* the Earth, seeing the visible through the template of the invisible. This second sense of logic requires the same rigorous clarity as the first, but also depends upon the ability (and opportunity!) to muse, entertain doubts, and withhold judgment, opening up the mental space necessary for things to reveal themselves as signs.

The importance of withholding judgment was apparent at Starved Rock, where Chris and the stranger crouched down and looked for fossils in the flagstone. Proof in such cases is improbable; I could only provide Chris with the beginnings of a *logos* ("Doesn't this have the organized look of something organic? See how it's patterned, with regularly repeated lines of structure? The elegant curve from tip to tip?"), and then invite him to enlarge his mind and create a space of possibility where the marks in the rock could mean something. Rather than seeing is believing, here was a case where one must at least believe in the possibility of something before one could see it. As for the other man, who saw nothing, it is of course possible that there was nothing to see. Certainly that is what he saw, nothing. But it may have been that the sources of authority in his life made it difficult to see those marks as the signs of past life.

The scene at Starved Rock illustrates the interplay of authority and reason in science. One element of Chris's conversion turned upon the authority he granted me as someone more knowledgeable in geology. Accounts of science commonly emphasize that authority plays no role in its deliberations; science distinguishes itself from other modes of life (e.g., religion) by relying exclusively upon evidential reasoning. But it turns out that authority plays a crucial role in the work of science. My faith in my advisor caused me to look again at bivalves that had seemed indistinguishable, just as students' trust in a professor or in the power of tradition can keep them laboring at a book that first seemed impossibly boring. Trust in a legitimate authority—scientific or otherwise—pries a mind open to consider new possibilities. Without it, there will not have been the suspension of disbelief needed for seeing what often, at first blush, seems unlikely and far-fetched.

This sense of authority is different from a unquestioned and unquestionable authority (in, say, fundamentalist religions); scientific authority remains provisional and transitory, eventually to be filled out and replaced by logic and evidential reasoning. If I were not able to make a reasonable case for the nonrandom nature of the shapes in the flagstone (for instance, by drawing upon other known facts consistent with my interpretation), Chris would have eventually rejected my authority. And as Martin Rudwick and others have noted, the appeal to authority plays a particularly central role in field science. Field experience is difficult or impossible to duplicate (outcrops are inaccessible, and in some cases disappear), and the scientific community depends especially on the trustworthiness of the reporter.[20]

The eye is not merely a receptor of data; vision both encapsulates and penetrates its object. Significant seeing includes a background or ambient awareness as well as focusing upon the object. The geologist asks pertinent questions of the outcrop by knowing his way around a topic, understanding it in an intuitive way. Geologic seeing depends upon the imaginative capacity to envision the outcrop, rather than the straightforward application of uniformitarian principles. Geologic seeing is poetic vision constrained by the sobriety of science, a series of daring imaginative leaps disciplined by examination and measurement. Defying the stereotypes of science, field geologists form a clan of surreptitious poets, their original aesthetic and metaphysical delight in landscapes still beating beneath their discipline's technical terms and laboratory apparatus. Rather than primarily driven by economics, geology is a type of walking meditation, a disciplining of the soul through the training of the eyes and body.

7

BEING AND GEOLOGIC TIME: THE MEETING OF METAPHYSICS AND POLITICS

What might geology look like in a postmodern era? In the modern era, geology was predominantly an economic discipline, supplying the raw materials needed for economic development. In the future, the central role of the Earth sciences should be political, helping to define the limits that individuals and communities must live within in order to flourish. These limits—mutable, and as motivated by aesthetics and metaphysics as by science and economics—will be best expressed as narratives that provide citizens with environmental contexts with which to script their lives. Embracing its nature as an explicitly narrative science, geology would not only create scientific knowledge, but also (with the help of humanists) place it into contexts that foster discussions about the common good.

I.

> The most thought-provoking thing about this thought-provoking time is that we're still not thinking.
>
> —Martin Heidegger

Heidegger's comment is unfair, of course. There has never been such an age of thinking. True, much of our thought now consists of calculating and measuring, planning and ordering—types of reasoning that for Heidegger do not rise to the level of *Denken*. But we also employ significant numbers of people to study such topics as ancient philosophy, medieval theology, and queer theory. What, then, is

117

Heidegger's complaint? And how can he claim that we so live under the sway of technology that it dominates all of our thinking?

Consider one of the stranger contrasts in recent culture, the Dalai Lama's 1997 appearance on CNN's *Larry King Live*. During the interview, King asked: "You recently said that we spend a lot of money on outer space and nothing on inner space. What do you mean?"[1] The Dalai Lama never quite answered the question—his response was cut short by a commercial. But we are at liberty to speculate on the topic. We may understand it as a comment on the basic character of the human condition: the world does not always give us what we want. There are two attitudes we may take toward this condition: modify our wants, or change the world so that it provides us with what we desire. The former choice embodies the wisdom of the ancient world, both East and West, which called upon us to fall into line with the nature of things. Both the individual and human society comprised microcosms to be modeled upon the macrocosm of nature. While manipulation of the world was far from unknown, *techné* (i.e., craft work) was subservient to *mimesis* (imitation) as man sought to mimic the natural order of things.

Since Bacon, Western civilization has championed the second alternative. We have become *Homo technologicus,* the being who manipulates both nature and self. This manipulation is not done according to a plan but is guided by the impulsive drive of the will. We no longer define progress as *Bildung,* the educational process of self-cultivation and self-mastery. Instead, we measure our success in terms of making the world more fully meet our desires. This technological imperative manifests itself as the ceaseless drive to increase the power and speed by which we place the world before us for manipulation. The apogee of this process—by which we bypass entirely the recalcitrance of matter—is virtual reality. But even before virtual reality, cable television and the World Wide Web enclose the world in a box on a table before us. Reality becomes instantly accessible, downloadable, and manipulable. And with genetic engineering, the malleability of reality according to our will is about to take another leap forward.

In a peculiar sense the West *has* mastered the art of controlling inner space—though not, probably, in the way the Dalai Lama imagined. Our fondness for chemical solutions—nicotine and caffeine, alcohol and marijuana, birth control pills and Viagra, Prozac and Xanax—constitutes the expansion of technology into the landscape of the self. Drugs are the tools of inner space, as consciousness itself becomes an artifact for our manipulation. Our culture's official attitude toward illicit drugs has an odd, anachronistic quality. While we embrace the manipulation of external nature, and indulge in all manner of chemical self-manipulation (through medicines), we resist acknowledging that drug users are merely applying the same logic to our mental landscapes. Perhaps some vestige of the natural still clings to our notion of personal identity, some sense that there are some places that should remain outside the ambit of manipulation. Of course, in some circles such talk is already passé. Retooling psychic space may soon be described as both more satisfying and more "ecological" than external technology. For if we can satisfy our desires through a change in our mental landscape, there will be less need to modify our physical landscape, for instance by cutting down an old-growth forest for a new redwood deck.

Technology exists to serve our desires. One might characterize the quarrel between the ancients and the moderns as the choice between Buddhism and technology—between disciplining the self, or manipulating reality to satisfy our urges. Heidegger's point, however, is something more than this. For Heidegger, technology does not, in the first instance, mean the set of artifacts that have become such a salient part of contemporary life. Rather, our artifactual way of life is a metaphysical orientation concerning the nature of reality. The world (including the self) has become a set of resources that we manage in accordance with our wishes. Even our scientific definition of truth is fundamentally technological in nature; the laboratory, our paradigmatic instance of scientific truth, is a space where objects are constrained and manipulated. We have lost the sense that there is a natural order to the world, a way (Dharma, Tao, telos) in which things are meant to develop, which we have a prima facie duty to acknowledge and respect. Put differently, we have lost a sense of the proper, the assumption that things (including humans) are limited in terms of what they should or should not do or be. Now—as Nietzsche noted—anything is possible.

This is true in two senses. First, we no longer recognize an intrinsic moral or metaphysical limit to our actions, a given or natural end to our lives. We have become Sartreans, seeing ourselves as being in a state of radical freedom, free to manipulate the world and ourselves as we please. The default position in ethics today is that each of us should be able to do exactly as he or she pleases, answering only to ourselves, with the only proviso that pursuing our desires does not conflict with the right of others to do the same. We have lost any sense of a purpose in life that would provide a criterion for judging our actions.

Second, science and technology today live under the sign of infinity. Both have become infinite research projects, with no goal short of total understanding and complete control. The questions "Do we know enough?" and "Is our power sufficient?" have no meaning. Answering them would require an assumption other than the formal one of increasing our comprehension and power. But this is exactly what we lack. The technological imperative has become the demand for ever greater augmentation of understanding and power. In *Forbidden Knowledge,* Roger Shattuck notes how unusual this attitude is from a historical perspective: it has been a truism across cultures that wisdom consists in recognizing limits, and that overreaching leads to disaster.[2]

It is thus doubly ironic that this ever greater understanding and power is not *our* understanding and power: individuals today control little and comprehend less of the technologies that influence their lives. Technology confronts us as a world of anonymous and implacable systems that develop according to a logic of their own:

> [D]igital technology is the solvent leaching the glue out of old, much cherished social, political and business structures. . . . We are performing a great unwitting experiment that is changing our social structures, our governmental structures and our business structures. Everything, absolutely everything is up for grabs and nothing's going to make any sense at all for a couple of decades, so we may as well sit back and enjoy the ride.[3]

Sit back and enjoy the ride? It is remarkable that we can be so sanguine about our "great unwitting experiment." But few object to incessant technological and cultural innovation. Evidently, the overwhelming majority of our fellow citizens view this experiment as an inherently benign process.[4]

These two points—our abandoning of the belief in inherent limits, and our tremendous and continually increasing technological power—are essentially one and the same. Technology can become autonomous only when we lose our sense of limits, our sense of the natural. Our public conversations no longer focus on the question of the nature of the good life. Seeing this question as essentially unanswerable, we have privatized the question of the good, leaving each to define the good life in terms of his or her own chosen, idiosyncratic pleasures. But while this postmodern condition strikes some as an unalloyed good, it does raise a question: if we embrace *logos* without *telos*, order without a pregiven end, then how do we choose the goals that we as individuals and communities should pursue? "By choosing to do whatever we want" seems the obvious answer. But the question's logic leads in another direction. While our desires are granted a modicum of respect ("Well, if that's what you want . . ."), they carry no real weight. They are simply a set of brute facts, explained by the idiosyncrasies of personality—or by what was once called sociobiology, now known as evolutionary psychology. Or, on another reading (which comes to the same thing), our desires are seen as mere artifacts or cultural constructs. According to this view, "needs" are simply expressions of the latest advertising slogans, themselves understood as expressions of ideology and power. In either case, our desires have become fundamentally arbitrary—as Freud said, polymorphously perverse.

But can we function without a sense of the natural? Is it really possible to live a life in which we understand our desires as merely a set of evolutionary codes or consumer preferences? In his parable of the Madman, Nietzsche is typically taken to be celebrating the death of the proper. But as he foresaw, the death of God—i.e., the death of the proper, of limit, and the natural—raises as many questions as opportunities:

> The madman jumped into their midst and pierced them with his eyes. "Whither is God?" he cried; "I will tell you. *We have killed him*—you and I. All of us are his murderers. But how did we do this? How could we drink up the sea? Who gave us the sponge to wipe away the entire horizon? . . . What festivals of atonement, what sacred games shall we have to invent? Is not the greatness of this deed too great for us?[5]

Without a sense of the natural, the self is threatened with incoherence, as we lose the constancy of will to choose and stick to one thing rather than another. People drift from one role to another, trying on lifestyles like sets of clothes. People and projects are "fascinating," but are abandoned when they become difficult or inconvenient. After a series of such "star friendships" (the phrase is Nietzsche's) one comes to anticipate how the next relationship will end. The lack of any commitment beyond that of self-pleasure acts as an acid that eats away at the relationship from the very moment that it forms. Since even play requires tenacity, every relationship takes on an amorphous and incomplete quality as all parties watch for the first sign of vacillation.[6]

Some will see this as too severe a commentary on our situation. Much of contemporary culture—and contemporary philosophy—has reinterpreted and embraced this denaturalization of the self, re-christening it the "nomad self," the self without identity or borders.[7] This self is described as the site of surface stimulations, where we partake of intense but essentially temporary relationships, with no necessary or even important connection between one interest (or self) and the next. According to this view, we surf lifestyles and rela-tionships the way we surf TV channels or the Web—both society and self as improvisation and pastiche. The question arises, however, whether such a self truly has the capacity for pleasure. For it may be that, without the sense of direction provided by natural goals and limits, the individual eventually sinks into the ennui born of half-completed projects and abandoned goals.

Granting these concerns as real, we are faced with a conun-drum: in an age that dismisses metaphysics as illusory, where can we find a sense of the natural—a sense of limits and of the proper?

II.

Geology has an ambivalent cultural image. Equipped with a rock hammer or manning a drilling rig, the geologist exemplifies the view of the Earth as resource. Geology not only provides the ma-terials to keep the machines running, but also supplies the materi-als with which we build the machines. The traditional character of the geologist, however, also embodies a Rousseauistic ideal. For the search for energy or the study of ecosystems implies a life spent out-doors, tramping the wilderness, beyond the bounds of civilization. Indeed, this latter image is in ascendance today, precisely when the field geologist is becoming an anachronism within his own disci-pline. Popular culture (e.g., the movie *Jurassic Park*) portrays the geologist as a temporal Odysseus or Captain Cook, charting new worlds and discovering mythic creatures across time rather than space.

The Earth lies at the root of all economic activity. This is clear enough when we are considering petroleum, copper, or coal; but it's less obvious that corn is geologic in origin. Soils are formed through geologic processes over geologic periods of time: in the High Plains, some of the best soils in the planet consist of loess deposits, the prod-ucts of Pleistocene glaciers. Loess consists of silt layers, sometimes tens of feet thick, in areas that once bordered continental glaciers. In

the Pleistocene, glaciers ground the rock underneath into tiny particles known as rock flour. The glacier's melting edge then released
large amounts of silt, which was carried by the wind in huge dust
storms that deposited the silt in downwind areas. Today 25 percent of
the topsoil of the High Plains is seriously degraded, with large
amounts having washed down to the Gulf of Mexico in the 125 years
since European settlement—a permanent and irreplaceable loss,
from the perspective of human interests. Moreover, the groundwater
used to irrigate these crops is also Pleistocene in origin, fossil water
drawn from the Ogallala aquifer, the legacy of glaciers melting eighteen thousand years ago. It is estimated that at current rates of
drawdown the Ogallala aquifer will last another thirty to fifty years.[8]

But if geology is rooted in economics, it is also poetic and metaphysical in nature. As I tried to capture in earlier chapters, the historical geologist's work is unusually dependent upon the capacity to
dream. Of course, every human endeavor, and certainly every science, requires imagination and creativity. But geology embodies this
point in a singular way. It is too often forgotten that, when we look
at re-creations of dinosaurs and the environments they inhabited,
these rich interpretations are based upon an extended series of inferences drawn from fragments of crushed bone pulled from twisted
and fractured strata.

This process of dreaming the outcrop itself depends upon a type
of ontological disruption, for the discipline of geology, in its development from the field of mineralogy, displaced our human-scaled sense
of time. James Hutton's discovery of geologic time (1788)—a length
of time so expansive that he could imagine "no vestige of a beginning, no prospect of an end"—represents much more than an arith-
metic fact. To open ourselves to the possibility of making sense of an
outcrop requires a transformation in one's lived sense of time, and
thus of reality. As John McPhee has shown in a series of books on geology and geologists, walking the Earth and thinking in terms of
deep time profoundly affects the way one experiences the world.
What was taken as real becomes ephemeral, while the inconsequen-
tial becomes freighted with significance. Viewed geologically, building condominiums on a beachfront is akin to setting up lodging on
an iceberg; the very term "beachfront property" becomes an oxymoron. And commonplace acts such as tossing away a Styrofoam
container that briefly held a burger become absurd and even ob-
scene: we discard after a moment's convenience a part of the world's
shrinking petroleum inheritance that came down to us through a
150-million-year-process?[9]

In *Being and Time* Heidegger emphasizes the importance of what he calls the ontological difference. This is the difference between Being and beings—between our overall sense of the nature of reality and the particular things that make up that reality. Heidegger argues that our overall understanding of the nature of Being determines what counts as real. Heidegger puts particular emphasis upon the role of time in defining our sense of reality, claiming in *Being and Time* that: "[O]ur provisional aim is the interpretation of *time* as the possible horizon for any understanding whatsoever of Being."[10] Throughout his work Heidegger offers a historical account of the meaning of Being across Western culture, identifying a small set of fundamental determination of Being (as *physis, poeisis,* as produced by a creator God, and as object)[11] across the history of Western civilization. Each of these determinations of Being presuppose a certain understanding of time. For instance, the sense that real things are "objective," i.e., consist of objects constantly present, presupposes that time expresses itself in a series of discrete present moments, rather than, say, as a continual process of becoming in which things are both passing into and out of existence. Similarly, today we are held by a technological understanding of reality in which we view everything as standing in reserve, constantly present and ready for manipulation (e.g., instant news updates, cell phones and beepers, and so on).

While the particularities of Heidegger's account of the history of our understanding of Being may be disputed, his basic point is a profound one. Our sense of temporality (as ill-defined and unselfconscious as it may be) determines the type and manner of things that strike us as real. If, discounting history and historical experience, we define the real as that which can be reproduced upon demand, then the results of the experimental sciences will define reality. Those aspects of reality that resist or deny repetition (a political decision; a moment in the mountains when the light is just so) will be seen as subjective and unreal. Similarly, if we define reality in terms of the profits turned last quarter, then the current price for a barrel of oil is a realistic measure of its worth. But seen from a perspective informed by deep time, cheap oil becomes mad profligacy.

By reorienting our sense of time, geology presents us with an innovation in our sense of reality. It is thus curious that Heidegger, well versed in the science of his time—and friends with Heisenberg—did not explore geology's effect upon our sense of temporality. At the same time that Heidegger was formulating the insights that resulted in *Being and Time,* geologists gained their first accurate sense of the expanses of the Earth's history. Radiometric dating of rocks was first attempted by B. B. Boltwood, a Yale chemist, in 1907. Relying upon the half-life of uranium, Boltwood calculated the Earth's age as being between 410 million years and 2 billion years. By 1920, Earth scientists possessed accurate numbers (in the 4-billion-year range) for the Earth's history.[12]

Geologic time's effect, however, does not turn on the objective facts concerning a particular rock's age. In terms of our lived experience, it makes no difference whether the Earth's age is finally found to be 2 billion or 4 billion years old. In either case, we have utterly transcended our previously anthropocentric view of time. If the Earth is something like six thousand years old, humans fill most of history's canvas. If the world is hundreds of millions or billions of years old, clearly we are a small part of a much greater story. When we see ourselves as geologic phenomena, placed within a grand cosmological and geological narrative, our lives and our behavior take on a different color.

Such narratives don't exist only on the grand cosmological scale. They get their greatest grip upon our lives on the local level. Helping people place themselves in terms of both space and time is a powerful means for addressing environmental problems. If you live in Phoenix, understanding the basic hydrologic story of central Arizona—the irrigation efforts of the Hohokam, the drying up the Salt River west of the Mazatzal Mountains, and the huge periods of geologic time that it took to create the decidedly limited aquifer underlying the area—is a powerful first step in getting people and municipalities to change their behavior. Rather than trying to impress ethical principals upon people, such knowledge changes our experience of reality, and thus our behavior.

Geologists make geologic time conceivable through the use of metaphors. So, for instance, the Earth's history is compared with the twenty-four hours of a day, and the last five minutes before midnight correspond to the appearance of humankind. Similarly, we can repackage one million seconds as eleven days, and 1 billion seconds as thirty-two years. Metaphoric repackaging (in terms like Tertiary, Cretaceous, Jurassic, etc.) gives the geologist an intuitively understandable narrative framework for geologic time.

Incomprehension and irrelevance also pass into understanding and meaning at those points where human and geologic time intersect. Earthquakes, floods, hurricanes, and droughts are places where deep time erupts into our more familiar temporal rhythms.

These places of contact will become increasingly common as the pressure of population growth and technological potency make the intersection of human and geologic time into a common territory. Geo-economics and geometaphysics will come together in the place where all questions eventually play out, the communal place that we may call the geopolitical. When irrigation west of the one-hundredth meridian is no longer possible because the Ogallala aquifer has run dry, or development in southern Arizona is tied in knots by water shortages, we will have felt geologic time in the most palpable of ways.

Our culture is clearly attached to its technological orientation to reality, and the signs are that we will continue to embrace this world-view into the foreseeable future. Indeed, it is nearly impossible to participate in contemporary life without becoming implicated in this orientation to reality—taking up both the tools of this world and the attitudes that these tools presuppose. The pull of this sense of reality upon other cultures is also understandable, as others seek the advantages of a Western lifestyle, from health care to the Internet. It is possible, however, that another dispensation of Being will manifest itself, one that casts the dominance of *Homo technologicus* into high relief—an era in which we temper the technological imperative by recognizing the reality of limits, and we once again guide our lives by a sense of the proper and the natural. We face the fundamental question of whether we will continue with the current laissez-faire approach to scientific research, technological development, and consumerism, or whether we will learn to temper these expressions of our desires. The latter possibility, in which we honor both natural limits and technological development, could be termed the age of geology.

III.

The suggestion that the twenty-first century will be the age of geology rests on the claim that we are entering a period in which natural limits will be the defining question of culture.

Ecogeologic abundance has been the sine qua non of the modern era. It is impossible to separate the story of the rise of *Homo technologicus* from the effects of Columbus's discovery of the New World. At that time, immigrants were presented with what was, by all practical measures, an infinity of metals, timber, water, fish, farmland, and space. The effects of such abundance were pervasive: ecogeologic abundance encouraged a laissez-faire or libertarian attitude not only toward economics, but also toward ethics, politics, and theology. Modernity is the name of the period in which the characteristic institutions and intuitions of Western civilization—capitalism, democracy, Protestantism, and privatizing the question of the good—rested upon the abundance of space and resources needed for the untrammeled pursuit of one's desires. From economics to politics to religion, individualism became the watchword—all based upon geo-ecological abundance. Thus we find John Locke, in his *Second Treatise on Government* (one of the founding documents of American political culture), defending private property by claiming:

> Nor was this appropriation of any parcel of Land . . . any prejudice to any other Man, since there was still enough, and as good left. So that in effect, there was never the less left for others because of his enclosure for himself.[13]

This effective infinity of resources meant that the circumstances that had traditionally defined the realm of the political no longer applied. For under the normal conditions of politics, choices were made within what was largely a zero-sum game. One person's or group's gain meant another's loss—making it obvious to all that one's decisions affected the lives of others. The epistemology of the political realm has traditionally been constituted by this fact, encouraging people to resolve issues through the give-and-take of dialogue and compromise.

The libertarian tenets of modernist epistemology and pedagogy have also been based upon abundance. For instance, the method of analysis is an individualistic epistemology of external relations in which we understand entities in isolation from one another. Epistemology and pedagogy are married within the division of labor of academia, which despite the purported "radical" nature of the professorate still presupposes these modernist assumptions. Universities divide disciplines and divide them again, as specialization and expertise have become the defining character of knowledge. This cult of specialization manifests itself at both the undergraduate and graduate levels: the undergraduate major and the Ph.D. dissertation both define specialized knowledge as higher knowledge.

In contrast to this, an age of geology would be a postmodern era in which natural limits are allowed to reassert themselves. The idea of natural limits, embracing both the natural world and human nature, has two aspects. First, it entails that natural beings have their own characteristic ways about them that prima facie deserve honor and respect. Trees, salmon, and ecosystems all change in ways that allow us to apply the terms "healthy" and "diseased." The category of the natural thus includes the ideas of the proper, the sacred, and limit—for to develop in one of a limited set of characteristic ways implies that there are ways that the thing should not develop. It challenges our culture of infinity, which expresses itself as the assumption that every being (even our own genetic code) is an object to be examined and a resource to manipulate. Second, geology— meant in the sense of a *logos* of the Earth that includes geopoetics, geopolitics, geotheology, *and* geoscience—would become the discipline that takes as its subject defining the term of the natural. This (postmodern) sense of geology would be concerned with identifying the increasingly obvious limits of space and resources that society will face in the twenty-first century.

This account means to introduce a distinctive type of postmodernism. In particular, it challenges the explicitly antinaturalistic presumptions that have dominated most strains of postmodernism, which have declared nature and the natural dead. On these latter accounts, interpretation and textuality reign supreme as everything is transposed into an artifact for reconstruction. In one of the few dissents from such postmodernist orthodoxy, Albert Borgmann has argued that most of what flies under the banner of postmodernity is better characterized as "hypermodern." Rather than seriously challenging modernity, most postmodernists have simply followed modernist assumptions to their logical conclusions, promoting an ever more radical individualist epistemology and politics. These versions of postmodernity feature an emphasis upon self-invention, a fascination with technology and the spectacular, and the apotheosis of difference. Borgmann contrasts this hypermodernism with the idea of a postmodern realism that takes the category of nature (including human nature) seriously. In his interpretation of postmodernity, human nature expresses itself by developing "focal realities"—the mastering of craft skills (e.g., carpentry, horsemanship, gardening, and writing) that temper the soul while showing respect for the nature of things—and through communal rituals that bring people together to form and share a public space.[14]

Much of contemporary continental philosophy takes a dim view of any claims concerning the natural.[15] Nature is not an independently existing other, but is constituted by our practices within the world. Moreover, the natural world revealed by science is characterized by instability and chaotic and random change. The claim that some act is "natural" is therefore merely an expression of a particular political investment. Certainly, the world is a construct in any number of ways: human labor transforms both our consciousness and the world, and the language and categories that we think with color all of our experience. But we also may quiet ourselves, and listen to what the world presents to us. There is a recalcitrance to reality that, however much it is filtered through our perceptual and historical templates, exists as an other. The Grand Canyon has been interpreted in a variety of ways, and has been at different times ignored as well as celebrated. But the Grand Canyon exists, vibrant and full of significance. To claim otherwise is to commit a fallacy typical of people who spend too much time inside, reading books.

William Ophuls, in *Ecology and the Politics of Scarcity* (first edition, 1977; revised, 1992), offers a powerful account of the idea of natural limits in the sense of physical or ecological constraints.[16] Ophuls's argument is straightforward: our society's social and political institutions and its philosophic intuitions have been based upon ecogeological abundance, and this abundance is coming to an end. We must therefore undergo a thorough reorganization of our sense of self, of community, and of nature (both conceptually and in terms of their expression in our institutions). Ophuls begins his argument by summarizing the current evidence on population growth, food production, pollution, deforestation, and energy and mineral resources. He contends that the indicators for each of these topics point toward inescapable environmental limits. But more crucially, Ophuls argues that these factors are synergistically related. Thus, even if most of the predicted shortages fail to materialize, the "law of the minimum" means that the factor in least abundance will limit the growth of all the rest. So, for instance, even if we are able to stop population growth while developments in biotechnology increase the productivity of cereals, limits in energy supply—and thus in fertilizer—will make growth in food production untenable. If, in turn, we find a way to overcome limits in energy supply, we will face unacceptable levels of air and water pollution. In a culture predicated upon infinite growth, any way we turn, we face limits to growth.

But while Ophuls is postmodern in his focus upon limit as the twenty-first-century culture's defining category, he is thoroughly modernist in assuming that science defines the character of the real. He sets aside arguments based upon values, choosing instead to make his case from the "value-free" facts of science:

Philosophical, ethical, and spiritual arguments seem to appeal only to the converted. Hard-headed scientists, technologists, bureaucrats, and businesspeople—the men and women

who make the basic decisions that shape our futures—do not
often pay much attention to such arguments. If one is to
argue constructively with the people who incarnate our cultural and political norms, one must argue the case in their
own terms. This requires that one adopt a fundamentally
empirical and scientific or agnostic approach, putting aside
the question of values, at least temporarily. . . .[17]

The scarcity mentioned by Ophuls is a fact of the physical sciences,
not of psychology or politics, aesthetics, metaphysics, or theology.

Modern Malthusian arguments such as Ophuls's are common
within the environmentalist literature, and a significant percentage
of scientists and citizens share them. But there is no dearth of authors who diametrically oppose these views. These "Cornucopians"
envision a technological escape hatch to the limits predicted by the
neo-Malthusians. Julian Simon, a leading Cornucopian, argued that
"technology exists now to produce in virtually inexhaustible quantities just about all the products made by nature."[18] For Simon, there
are no naked geologies, no bare natural facts of the matter. Geologic
facts are themselves constructions of technology: "We have in our
hands now . . . the technology to feed, clothe, and supply energy to an
ever-growing population for the next seven billion years."[19] To take
one prominent example, world oil reserves continue to increase despite our use of them, because technology steadily improves in discovering new sources and drawing more from old ones. In Simon's
view, physical limits simply reflect the current state of human inge-
nuity; human inventiveness is the "ultimate resource" that makes
all other resources infinite.[20] The environmental economist Mark
Sagoff has recently made a similar claim. Citing a wide variety of
technological advances in the recovery of raw materials, the development of cereal crops and aquaculture, and advances in tree farming, he declares: "It is simply wrong to believe that nature sets
physical limits to economic growth."[21]

Now, Ophuls recognizes that technological advance presents the
main challenge to his Malthusian account of our future. He devotes
considerable attention to whether technology will enable us to overcome natural limits. His argument turns on three points. First, he
decouples scientific knowledge from its technical application. While
granting that acquiring scientific knowledge is a potentially infinite
process, he argues that this does not guarantee that science will continue to be translated into useful technical information. Second,
even if we come up with technological solutions, we will still press up

against various financial, organizational, or temporal obstacles to implementing these solutions. The history of nuclear power in the United States provides examples of the pitfalls in each of these areas. Third, Ophuls notes the tension, and even the incompatibility, between technology and democracy: insofar as technology becomes more complex, it becomes more difficult for the average citizen to make an informed decision concerning its use. In Ophuls's account, even if science and technology were to succeed in overcoming the limits we face, it would be a Pyrrhic victory.

Confronted by this welter of claims and counterclaims, Theodore Roszak takes a different tack on the debate between the Malthusians and the Cornucopians. On nearly every environmental issue today, different sides are able to marshal scientific evidence that supports their views. To Roszak, the dilemma of dueling experts only highlights our radical epistemological uncertainty. Science is simply incapable of giving us an unequivocal answer to the environmental questions we pose. "We count and measure, measure and count again. But do we have the right numbers? Do we have enough numbers?"[22] Given our experience to date, Roszak questions our faith that further science will resolve rather than exacerbate the uncertainties surrounding our future.

Roszak suggests that it is time to reorient the environmental debate away from questions of environmental science and toward a concern with psychology and the nature of human satisfaction. Roszak offers a post-Freudian account of psychology that locates the unconscious in the natural world, rather than within the recesses of the human mind. In an argument reminiscent of Paul Shepard's work, Roszak describes how our psychic lives evolved in concert with the sounds and rhythms of nature—daylight and darkness, the turn of the seasons, and our intimate relation to plants and animals.[23] Roszak argues that our habits of abusing nature, as well as our pattern of overconsumption, betray a sickness of the soul rooted in our estrangement from the natural world. The roots of this sickness lie in modernism's account of a dead and purposeless universe. (Roszak devotes considerable energy to questioning modern science's claim that life and the universe consist of sound and fury signifying nothing.) In taking over this account, modern psychology made it irrational to care for the world. The result is that we left ourselves with only a cultural or conventional basis for defining sanity, based upon the individual's adaptation to society.

Roszak makes a signal contribution to the environmental debate by turning us toward questions of psychology rather than science, and meaning rather than fact. But while raising the indispensable question of how sanely we have treated the Earth, Roszak overstates the degree of uncertainty surrounding the scientific assessment of environmental issues. There is today a fair degree of consensus concerning a number of environmental issues, from global climate change to the future of recoverable oil reserves. Roszak seems to assume that science can only inform public policy decisions through its predictive certainty. Missing from his account of science is Aristotle's sense of *phronesis* or practical wisdom. *Phronesis* is essentially a conservative approach to questions of public concern, a conservatism rooted in recognizing the fragility of community and the irreversibility of the historical process. It identifies our capacity to reason about social or political questions that are not susceptible to calculative reason. The ability to *deliberate*—to weigh and consider, to ponder and reflect and reach a consensus through the give-and-take of conversation—was once understood as the epistemology appropriate to political debate. In ancient Greece, the *polis* provided the social space for deliberative dialogue among citizens.

The work of Ophuls contains one element of a larger environmental philosophy, and that of Roszak, another; what is missing is the marriage between these two perspectives. By melding these two perspectives, we may gain a realistic understanding of the type of geologic scarcity that we will face. Both the Malthusians and Cornucopians have read scarcity along modernist lines, as indicating the physical absence of a resource. Ecogeologic scarcity was a "pure given," beyond human interpretation, and thus beyond the boundaries of value. But as Roszak suggests, the scarcity we will face will be as much a psychological and spiritual phenomenon as a physical one. As we experience the stresses (psychological, aesthetic, theological) of too many people, too much congestion, and too many demands on our time, our experiential sense of scarcity will play as large a part in our political debates as material scarcity.

Consider the case of Arches National Park in Utah. In 1989, the National Park Service established the VERP (Visitor Experience and Resource Protection) program at Arches. The goal of VERP was to identify the point at which the visitor's experience and the park's natural resources were unduly affected by the presence of too many people. As part of this program, the park asked visitors to look at a series of computer-generated pictures of the trail running out to Delicate Arch. The Park Service used this data for subsequent park management plans. For instance, it redesigned (and shrank) the Delicate Arch trailhead parking lot to limit the number of hikers to the site. In its account of this program, the Park Service emphasizes issues such as the carrying capacity of the land and how trail overuse can damage the vegetation and the soil along the shoulders of park roads.[24] Tellingly, while the importance of "visitor experience" is noted, the Park Service does not analyze the term, and certainly doesn't discuss the aesthetic and theological motivations that motivate many of the Park's visitors. Once again, aesthetic or theological concerns have been translated into the language of science or economics.

Geologic scarcity must be understood in a postmodern fashion. Scarcity and limit are simultaneously natural and cultural concepts, marking the interplay of physical limits—always uncertain, and subject to change through new discoveries and technological advance—and a complex range of cultural limits involving economics, ethics (questions of justice), aesthetics (quality-of-life issues), and theology (a sense of the sacred). As I have noted earlier, the interdisciplinary nature of environmental issues has already affected the discipline of geology. It has become a commonplace within the geoscience community to replace the term "geology" with "Earth science" or "Earth systems science." These new terms were coined to express the recognition that nature is an integrated whole that we must approach through a combined examination of the atmosphere, hydrosphere, lithosphere, and biosphere. Understanding issues such as global warming or the loss of biodiversity requires the combined efforts of atmospheric physicists, oceanographers, paleoclimatologists, and biologists.

But the redefinition of geology has paused before the next and, in my opinion, inevitable step. In holding to the older term "geology," I have tried to emphasize that we must see limit as simultaneously scientific, economic, political, aesthetic, and theological in nature. The original sense of "geology" emphasizes this point. A truly integrated *Geo-logos* would recognize that we must treat these various perspectives on the Earth as complementary rather than opposed. In brief, the Earth sciences must begin to integrate the humanistic and political as well as the scientific aspects of their discipline. But how, practically, are we going to accomplish this?

IV.

The political expression of limit is authority. Authority—defined as the legitimate exercise of power over others—is nearly an anachronism in our culture, a victim of the democratic and scientistic spirit of the age. Nothing characterizes modernity better than scientism, the belief that the scientific method defines the realm of truth, and that traditional ways of knowing (e.g., philosophy, religion, art) are chimerical. Our culture's acceptance of scientism has made suspect anything other than scientific authority, and libertarianism the default position on matters beyond the bounds of science. Since it is impossible to reason about claims made in ethics, politics, aesthetics, or theology, authority in these fields is inherently illegitimate. The only reasonable political attitude is that everyone should be as free from control as is humanly possible.

For all their differences, the political left and right today share a root libertarian impulse. The difference is that each applies libertarianism to a different arena of contemporary life. A mark of the libertarian position's success is that each side wins when it argues from libertarian grounds: the right in terms of economics, the left in cultural matters. The demand for less control has been successful in both economics and personal morality. Questions concerning the nature of the good life have become privatized—a result rooted in Descartes's rejection of the Aristotelian model of knowing, in which the intellectual virtues include *phronesis* and *nous* (intuitive reason) as well as *epistemé* (scientific knowledge).[25]

The question facing us is whether libertarianism remains tenable in an age of geologic scarcity. I believe that it does not. We must relegitimize moral limits and political authority in order to contend with the challenges we face. One step toward invigorating limit and authority within our culture lies in moderately reconfiguring the role of the public scientist. A restructured (or postmodernist, in Borgmann's sense of the term) discipline of the Earth sciences offers the means to revitalize moral limit and political authority. It may help to bring the reign of *Homo technologicus* to a close. To explain this claim, I offer an account of the U.S. Geological Survey, the nation's oldest Earth science agency. In terms of the federal government, the USGS is a relatively small organization, with ten thousand employees and a 850 million dollar annual budget (by comparison, NASA's 2002 research and development budget was almost ten billion). Nonetheless, as I will show in the next chapter, the agency's history highlights the political and philosophic dimensions of Earth science information and perspectives, and stands as a token of the possibilities inherent within public or political science.

8

SCIENCE AND THE PUBLIC SELF

We sit in Ken Mayfield's twentieth-floor office. It is May of 2001.
The city of Vancouver sprawls before us; just beyond lie the Straits
of Georgia and the mountains of British Columbia. Ken is a senior
artist at Lunny Communications Group, a Vancouver multimedia
firm that has spent the last few months turning data from the Geological Survey of Canada (GSC) into virtual reality. Sitting us before
a computer monitor, Ken leads us on a virtual tour of the Georgia
Basin (GL:CH8).

Pivoting the mouse around an imaginary point in the sky, we
zoom in and out on the landscape of western Canada. Howe Sound
comes into view; we fly up the fjord, soaring above the mountains of
British Columbia. As we pass over this virtual world, the bottom third
of the screen offers a map view that locates us within the landscape.
As we move across the simulated geography, hypertext markers appear. Click on one, and a text box opens to discuss such features as the
Britannia Mine and its problems with acid mine drainage. In the
summer of 2001, this virtual tour of the Georgia Basin could be ac-
cessed from a helicopter cockpit at Science World, the Vancouver children's science museum. Children now tour the region via mouse,
viewing the world through a set of monitors placed in the cockpit.

This project (and its companion effort in community planning,
known as the Georgia Basin Futures Project)[1] typifies the new role
that Earth science information and public science agencies are playing in society. It no longer suffices to throw scientific results over the
wall separating science from society. Today, science must be placed
in contexts nonspecialists can understand. What is more, the conversation between public science and society must be a true dialogue, with the scientific community listening to as well as
instructing society. The GSC and the U.S. Geological Survey have
discovered that scientific information is not, by its very existence,

necessarily relevant to anyone. These agencies are coming to acknowledge two distinct responsibilities: to produce impartial, high-
quality scientific information, *and* to place that information within
the variety of societal contexts helpful to policy makers, private
industry, and citizen's groups.

Recognizing this dual charge, however, has given birth to a
whole series of questions. The changing demands made upon the
GSC and the USGS offer yet another example of the ontological disruption affecting both intellectual culture and society at large. Is it
proper for scientists to engage in "political" activities? Won't such efforts undermine the uniquely objective status of scientific information? What is the role of public science agencies in negotiating the
boundaries between science and society? And, what do we make of
attempts such as the virtual display at Science World? Do they bring
us closer to the natural world, or are they a distraction, replacing
the environment with a virtual world so seductive that it relieves us
of the need to go outside at all?

This mix of scientific, political, and metaphysical concerns have
become deeply intertwined in public debates over public science. The
questions raised above are the subject of sustained—and sometimes
rancorous—debates within the GSC and the USGS, as these agencies struggle to define the proper range of public science. But before
turning to these issues, let us review the background of this disruption in categories.

I.

In 1995, the 104th Congress abolished the Bureau of Mines, a
$140 million federal science agency concerned with environmental
geology and mine safety. In the same session, Congress came within
a few votes of eliminating the U.S. Geological Survey. The USGS
conducts research on a wide range of topics. It analyzes earthquakes, provides mineral and energy assessment, water monitoring, and biological surveys, and identifies natural hazards. While
the Survey survived the vote in Congress, it was not without cost.
In the reorganization that followed, the Geologic Division of the
USGS lost 525 jobs.[2]

On several grounds, congressional critics questioned the need
for these agencies. First, they were concerned with the relevance of
the scientific research. How did studies in paleontology, hydrology,
or deep mantle processes serve the needs of the nation? Second was

the question of uniqueness. Why do we need a public science agency, when private companies could more efficiently handle those aspects of research that were relevant? Privatization had worked in other areas of government; if an area of research (say, an assessment of the nation's reserves in oil and gas, or a study of the health of an ecosystem) were truly useful, wouldn't there be a market for the information? Third, critics raised questions about the objectivity of the research being done. Were agency scientists guilty of promoting their own values under the guise of disinterested science?

While congressional critics were not casting their concerns in the language of political philosophy, they were broaching an issue whose roots go back to Plato. Their question was at once epistemological and political: What is the relation between governance and knowledge? Agencies such as the USGS, NASA, the Department of Agriculture's Agricultural Research Service, and the Commerce Department's National Institute for Occupational Safety and Health represent a wide-ranging federal commitment to public research. But what justifies this commitment? Are some aspects of knowledge crucial to the public, and liable to be abused or neglected if left in private hands? And if such research must be housed within government, how can public science agencies avoid the following contradiction: once their work becomes relevant to public concerns, it is precisely at that moment that the work is seen as having lost its vaunted objectivity?

The relation of knowledge and democracy has troubled thinkers since the founding of the American Republic. Early chapters of this debate included the Lewis and Clark Expedition, the possible creation of a national university, and whether to accept—and how to use—John Smithson's gift for the creation of an institution intended for "the increase and diffusion of knowledge among men." The issue was, in the first instance, legal. The only mention of science in the Constitution concerned patents that Congress "shall . . . promote the Progress of Science and useful Arts, by securing for limited Times to Authors and Inventors the exclusive Right to their respective Writings and Discoveries."[3] Federal support for science was legitimized by *McCulloch v. Maryland* (1819), when Chief Justice John Marshall affirmed the constitutional doctrine of implied powers, which gave Congress not only the powers expressly conferred upon it by the Constitution, but also whatever authority it needed to carry out such powers. Later chapters of this debate include the 1862 founding of the Department of Agriculture, and the 1950 creation of the National Science Foundation, a public agency devoted to funding fundamental scientific research.[4] In all of these discussions, critics questioned the legitimacy of the government's being involved in the production of knowledge. The 1995 congressional debates surrounding the BLM and the USGS resurrected these ghosts. The question now was whether such research should be privatized, either by turning the research over to academics and private industry, or by funding universities to conduct the research through such agencies as the National Science Foundation and the National Institutes of Health.

The question of the relation between knowledge, government, and democracy has been a perennial one within American culture. In a political culture born of the Enlightenment's rejection of traditional claims to authority based in heredity, military power, or religion, the federal government was bound to be drawn into the production of knowledge. In Enlightenment cultures, knowledge has been the fundamental way to legitimate decision-making. Of course, populist proponents of pure democratic self-expression challenged the claim that political legitimacy should be based in knowledge or expertise. But others argued that the democratic expression of opinion is meaningless and even dangerous without the constraints of education. Indeed, this latter point provided the initial justification for compulsory education (rather than the economic benefits of schooling). An educated electorate was understood to be crucial to a properly functioning democracy.

In a curious case of unintended consequences, the antiauthoritarian attitude typical of American democracy served to strengthen the authority of (especially scientific) knowledge. The Founding Fathers sought much more than a simple substitution of a president for a king; American government was founded upon a conservative political philosophy that distrusted authority. American institutions were designed to impede politicians' ability to make decisions.[5] This philosophy underlies the distribution of power across three branches of government and between local, state, and federal powers, and the existence of devices like short terms of office for members of the U.S. House of Representatives. Even the design of the nation's capital expressed a political point: in order to de-emphasize the presidency's power, the National Mall culminates in the Capitol rather than in the president's home. The net result has been that an inexperienced political class has often found itself depending on the more permanent class of intellectuals (e.g., university presidents, scientific committees such as the National Academy of Science, and think tanks) for the ideas underlying governmental policies.

The Enlightenment attitude that approached knowledge as the vehicle of political legitimization was greatly augmented by cultural developments of the nineteenth and twentieth centuries. The industrial revolution and the growth of cities in the United States (by 1859, less than half of the populace lived on farms) led to demands for governmental standards in areas such as sanitation, engine boilers, and fire and building codes. Industry had become extraordinarily large, in terms of both its economic power and its regional and national scope. Only the federal government had the resources and national reach to counterbalance this industrial might. The need for federal regulations, in turn, spurred the creation of federal science agencies. If they were not going to be seen as arbitrary, these regulations needed to be based upon scientific research. And if these results were not going to be simply dismissed as partisan—science captured by special interests—the science must be produced as part of the public trust.

Public science was thus created in recognition of the fact that knowledge is power. In fact, some knowledge is so crucial to societal decision-making that it cannot be privatized without compromising the public realm. In this sense, knowledge is similar to national defense—or for that matter, the local police force. Both must held as part of the public trust. We find, then, the first of two fundamental reasons that underlie the necessity of federal science agencies: society's need for honest brokers, researchers whose interests are explicitly tied to motives of the common good rather than to private interest.

The fundamentally *political* nature of this responsibility bears emphasizing: the concept of the common good must not be reduced to economic well-being. Public science agencies are distinctive in that they serve those aspects of our lives that either *should not* or *cannot* be turned into relations of economics—because the information is too crucial to be safe in private hands, or because there is no market for the information. The increasingly common habit of speaking of the public as *customers* or *consumers* of public science is understandable, being motivated by a desire to emphasize that public scientists have obligations to the public. But it is precisely wrong. It destroys the root justification for public science agencies. For rather than simply serving existing prejudices (as is the case with consumer preferences, where the customer is always right), public science agencies exist to inform and raise the level of public debate within a democracy.

In truth, it should be noted that economic metaphors for the functioning of government do not originate with public science agencies. Rather, this language is merely a symptom of a larger habit across political culture. Calls for "running government like a business" are common across both parties. While this is sometimes merely code for government being as efficient as possible, such rhetoric betrays a profound misunderstanding of the nature of the political realm. Politics is, at least at times, about transcending self-interest in order to make sacrifices for the good of community and nation.

There is a second reason underlying public science agencies, beyond that of serving as honest brokers of information too critical to be left in private hands. Public agencies are also needed in order to gather information on topics whose spatial or temporal scope exceeds market mechanisms. This second role of public science is based in the diffuseness of some types of knowledge. Some vital knowledge is likely to be marginalized or ignored through "market failure," either because the information cuts across a wide range of space or institutions, or because it will not likely become relevant until some indefinite time in the future. Monitoring the nation's rivers and streams is clearly in the interest of the various communities that live near or depend on them, but no private concern is likely to make significant investments in gathering this information. Into the breach steps the USGS, which maintains 8,000 gauging stations nationwide. Of course, insurance companies exist to cover risks that often extend long into the future. But such companies cover the possibility of already known and calculable risks. They don't engage in research into possible new hazards.

These two points only begin to give an account of public science agencies' distinctive responsibilities. Not only must we understand the unique place of agencies such as the USGS in the production of knowledge, but we must also appreciate the democratic responsibilities of these agencies to provide pertinent contexts for the information they discover. The U.S. Geological Survey offers us a useful case study of both, the traditional and the new functions of public science agencies.

II.

The tension noted earlier between two visions of geology—as exclusively economic in nature, or as including political as well as aesthetic and theological dimensions—runs through the history of the U.S. Geological Survey. Founded in 1879, the USGS grew out of the military and civilian land surveys that mapped the vast lands of the West. The original charter of the USGS called for the "classification of the public lands, and examination of the geological structure, mineral resources, and products of the national domain."[6] Clarence King, the USGS's first director, personified the economic interpretation of this mission. Early Survey work centered on studying the origin of ore deposits and mapping the mineral districts in Colorado (Leadville) and Nevada (the Comstock). King, however, left office after only eighteen months, presenting the second director, John Wesley Powell, with the opportunity to redirect the USGS toward a more politically and even philosophically oriented role in society. The range of Powell's interests is reflected by the fact that, during and after his thirteen-year tenure at the USGS, he also directed the U.S. Bureau of Ethnology. As its director, Powell guided the creation of the bureau's two-volume *Handbook of American Indians*, the groundbreaking summary of Amerindian cultures published shortly after his death.[7]

In contrast to King, Powell saw geology lying at the intersection of nature and culture, at a site he called the "geosocial." In his view, geological and hydrological questions naturally flowed into issues of land use policy, anthropology, and philosophy. The natural and cultural worlds were discrete, but continually intersected with one another. Moreover, Powell believed that civil servants can inform public decision-making and provide guidance to democratic decision-making. He espoused a strong model of governance: politicians and civil servants should not merely reflect community values, but should rather take a leadership role in the forming of public policy. Michael Sandel has called this the republican model of governance; the voters' role is to select the candidate whose outlook is most consistent with their own, and then allow him or her to govern. Voters retain ultimate control, for at term's end they may choose to remove the office-holder. Sandel contrasts this with the representative model of rule, in which the elected official mirrors the voters' views, no matter how inconstant, and the civil servant functions simply as a *servant*, following the views of the body politic rather than being in dynamic interaction with them.[8] It is, of course, the representative model that is exemplified by the poll-driven politics of current political life.

Powell's notion of the geosocial is clearly present in his 1878 *Report of the Lands of the Arid Region*. Water—or the lack of it—is the central fact of Western life, destined to affect the region's style of human settlement. The new culture of the West begins at the one-hundredth meridian, the line of longitude running through western

North Dakota and South Dakota and down through Kansas, Okla-
homa, and Texas that marks the isohyetal line of twenty inches of
annual rainfall, the minimum amount needed for unirrigated crops.[9]
West of this line, farming and settlement depend upon streams,
groundwater, and technology.

Powell saw the USGS as helping to create a "drylands democracy" that configured itself to the conditions on America's arid lands.
In this spirit, he was the inspiration behind the 1888 federal statute
that mandated the completion of an irrigation survey of all public
lands in the arid regions before they were opened to public settlement. Powell's irrigation survey would identify the water resources
throughout the West. Local, state, and federal governments would
then use this information for the rational design of communities.
While Powell had a strong utilitarian streak, believing that natural
resources should serve the people's needs, gathering and using this
information was more than simply a point of Taylorist efficiency.
Scarce resources invariably invited monopolies to corner markets. If
there was not enough rain for crops to grow, then whoever controlled
the water sources controlled the entire region. Powell's goal was to
place the results of the irrigation survey in the public domain, available to all, thereby encouraging political discussion and rational
planning. His point of view is encapsulated by his insistence that
state boundaries should follow the natural boundaries of water-
sheds, rather than the abstract lines of a Cartesian grid laid out on
a map in Washington, D.C.

Enacted by Congress in 1888, Powell's irrigation survey soon
ran into stiff political opposition. In 1890, the law was repealed by a
combination of Western money interests, advocates of small government, and the era's general land-rush mentality. In 1891, and again
in 1892, the Survey's funding was slashed as a sign of congressional
displeasure. Powell's own salary was cut as well. Powell resigned,
and the Survey retreated, reaffirming its role as public servant, and
returning to a fundamentally economic understanding of its mission.
Within the Survey, Powell was seen as having nearly destroyed the
organization by willfully disobeying the people's representatives—
rather than seen as having been engaged in a legitimate and noble
(if ill-fated) political exercise.[10]

The upshot of this controversy was to short-circuit public debate about the unique societal position of agencies such as the
USGS. In addition to his willfulness—for Powell was not as politic
with senators as he might have been—Powell's failure was ascribed
to his attempt to direct the Survey toward investigations that were

too theoretical in nature and better suited to universities. The Survey's third director, Charles Walcott, is seen as having properly reoriented the Survey's work toward the nation's practical needs. But this miscasts the debate. Powell was not primarily interested in pursuing theoretical science. Rather, he wanted to create a federal Earth science agency that functioned as something more than a public lackey. Powell's USGS sought to be the sensing organ of the body politic, but it would not stop there. The USGS was to be an advocate for the public good.

Is such a vision relevant today? In an era characterized by the belief in rampant subjectivism on questions of value, and dazzled by claims of "difference" (political, cultural, and sexual), an appeal to the notion of a common good can seem anachronistic and naïve—or authoritarian. The USGS's role is further circumscribed by longstanding philosophical commitments that see science alone as providing objective knowledge. But these objections miss the point. The idea of a public life without the idea of a common good itself depends on the effective infinity of natural resources—a situation now coming to an end. Under conditions of natural limit—the parameters of which the discipline of geology will describe, in rough outline—we need a rough consensus on a wide range of societal issues. Given these conditions, few people will embrace the utter relativity of ethical judgments. Indeed, it is often those within the social constructivist camp who clamor most insistently for environmental justice.

The USGS experienced steady growth throughout the early and mid twentieth century, greatly benefiting from expanded public funding for science after World War II. But the increase in funding did not lead to a more nuanced sense of the complex relationship between science and politics. Moreover, talk of natural limits was at low ebb. The environmental movement lay in the future. Survey work came to be characterized by a Lone Ranger mentality, in which a Survey scientist chose a topic of scientific research according to his or her own interests. Isolation from the political realm and its controversies was seen as a sign of the integrity of Survey science, a token of its lack of an agenda and thus a marker of its objectivity.

By the mid-1980s, however, the Survey budgets had flattened, and the USGS found itself squeezed by a shift in social tectonics. Two features had changed. First was the fact that the Survey's original mission—mapping and identifying the nation's natural endowment—was largely complete. New discoveries would be made, and maps would need revising, but the great era of geologic discovery (at least in the United States) was over.[11] Second, geology had become inescapably tied to political and philosophical issues. In earlier times, with a smaller population, less concern with pollution, and a national consensus on the desirability of economic growth, it was possible to ignore Powell's charge to the Survey. That is, a geologist's work could be limited to scientific issues such as identifying the grade and tonnage of a copper deposit. But by the 1980s, the very act of energy and mineral exploration had become controversial. Proponents of other values such as human health, the preservation and enhancement of community, the protection of biodiversity, and the desire for natural beauty grew more insistent in asking, what was the point of economic growth if it actually impoverished our lives?

The 1994 midterm elections overwhelmed the incipient debate within the Survey over its proper role in society. Claiming that any truly useful function of the USGS could be privatized, the Republican "Contract With America" called for eliminating the USGS as well as of the U.S. Bureau of Mines. The USGS thus found itself caught between twin dangers. Hewing to scientific objectivity opened it to charges of irrelevance, but if it tried to demonstrate its importance to society, it was liable to be drawn into political controversies. The dilemma facing the Survey was and remains: Can it provide the guidance that communities and the nation need without losing its status as the provider of impartial and credible scientific information?

III.

More than any other figure in contemporary culture, the scientist functions as the arbiter of truth. The debate over global climate change is shaped by the conclusions reached by the U.S. Global Change Research Program, just as the data informing the acid mine drainage controversy in the San Juans has been generated by the U.S. Geological Survey. There are, of course, experts in many other professions, such as law and the military, but even these fields are becoming ever more dependent upon science. The explosive growth of scientific knowledge constantly spawns new experts and domains of knowledge. At the same time, this flood of facts makes it progressively more difficult to gain a synoptic understanding of a problem. The growth of knowledge thus stymies democratic decision-making as much as it promotes it.

In 2002, the U.S. federal government spent more than 40 billion dollars on non-defense-related scientific research—30 percent of all scientific research conducted within the United States. When we narrow the focus to basic research, government funding jumps to 60 percent of the total.[12] Publicly funded science is conducted by industrial firms working under government contracts, by professors at colleges and universities working under government grants, and by national labs such as the Jet Propulsion Laboratory (JPL) and National Renewable Energy Lab (NREL). In each of these venues, publicly funded science treads a distinctive border region lying between science and the political realm.

As noted above, the scientist's traditional embrace of value-free objectivity has reached an impasse, both epistemologically and politically. This has placed scientists in public agencies in a singular position. The accustomed posture of the scientist vis-à-vis the body politic has been one of principled distance from the values that interest groups seek to impose on scientific knowledge. Whether it was an industry association, or an environmental organization like the Sierra Club, the scientist stood apart. It has been a point of honor that scientist's work remain value-free, preserving the integrity of science and thereby allowing science to contribute impartially to societal debates.

This stance has a number of attractive elements, not the least of which is that it protected scientists from being drawn into political contestations. But such studied neutrality has now been challenged on multiple fronts. Philosophers of science have found such a stance to be problematic, in that every investigation is fundamentally shaped by values of one type of another.[13] Even more striking is the fact that the very stance of principled distance from societal debates has opened the public scientist to charges of irrelevance. But neither is it acceptable for government scientists to slip into a stance of advocacy, in which they use their positions to advocate their personal views on a subject. How, then, does the public scientist negotiate the twin dangers of irrelevance and bias?

Resolving this predicament turns on our critically examining the sense of self that underlies the current debate over the scientist's role in society. Indeed, our society's notion of the self has a decided effect upon *all* political conversations. When scientists enter the public realm in order to advocate positions based upon their research, it is presumed that they have stepped beyond the ordinary bounds of science and lost the objectivity that is crucial to their good names as scientists. Advocacy of any type is taken as simply the expression of personal opinion. But while we certainly can find examples where this is the case, to label all advocacy by public scientists as inherently improper misunderstands the role that public science can and must play in the life of our culture.

The belief that advocacy is inappropriate for public scientists itself depends upon the metaphysical claim that selfhood is a unitary phenomenon. Indeed, our culture defines all senses of the self as personal and subjective, and thus opposed to true, objective knowledge. The contrast is especially strong in the case of science, where scientists supposedly enter into a selfless realm of objectivity upon entering the lab. A more nuanced account of the self sees it as consisting of two parts—a public and a private self. Whether as a schoolteacher, a tax accountant, or a soccer coach, we all inhabit roles that require us to act differently than we would as private individuals. Overlooking this elemental social experience gives birth to the scientist's, and especially the public scientist's, dilemma.

The loss of this distinction shows up in contemporary descriptions of the relation between the individual and the government. Politicians declare that the government should give back our money, because we know better how to spend it than does government. But back from whom? Government has come to be viewed as radically Other, a distant and hostile entity, rather than as an extension of oneself. The point is not simply that politicians will often use the public's money in ways to benefit themselves, or on pork-barrel projects in their home districts. Rather, we seem to have lost any sense of identification with our government, especially the federal government. Democratic government's founding principle, the view of government as the embodiment of a special dimension of the self, has fallen out of public favor. Perhaps this is the inevitable result of life in the modern nation-state. To take the example of the United States, alienation from the body politic is understandable in a country with a population of nearly 300 million. But if we wish to avoid this melancholy conclusion, we need to awaken a richer sense of the self, one part private, the other public, each having distinctive relations with and responsibilities to the community.

A public sense of self implies something more than simply the public role or persona of highly visible people. All of us take up a variety of roles in our many relationships. Distinguishing between our public and private selves is an exercise in approximation: any realistic account of the public and private self must admit of gradations. The self can be parsed to distinguish between our solitary lives, our family lives, our public selves within privately owned companies, our roles within public institutions such as universities or city governments, and finally our responsibilities as politicians or public officials. A more nuanced conception of selfhood helps us identify our distinct responsibilities in the many roles we play. More particularly, a richer conception of selfhood offers public scientists a way to give guidance to the community without simply being viewed as expressing personal points of view.

Consider two examples. First, within our legal system, the distinction between the public and private self is fundamental to the lawyer's role. Our judicial system is founded upon an adversarial philosophy, presuming that the search for truth is best achieved by presenting the strongest possible clash of views to a judge and jury. Lawyers will on occasion find that they have been assigned to defend clients or positions that they find odious. But as officers of the court, lawyers have an explicit obligation to set aside personal opinions and defend their clients' interests. In the language of the legal profession's Canon of Ethics, the lawyer must exhibit "entire devotion to the interests of the client, [and] warm zeal in the maintenance and defense of his rights."[14]

Second, consider the situation of a volcanologist working for the U.S. Geological Survey in the Pacific Northwest. Her research reveals a significant chance that a volcanic eruption would produce a lahar (a catastrophic release of mud, ice, and debris), presenting a credible risk to a populated area of Washington State. The scientist's personal preference is to remain out of the public eye: she is of a retiring nature, and furthermore seeks no controversy with either her employer or segments of the public (e.g., the business community). But a sense of public responsibility leads the her to place her findings not only in professional journals but also in popular publications. Over the next year, she attends meetings of the local and state government and engages in public debate in various community settings. In these debates, she raises the possibility of measures such as the public purchase and demolition of homes and businesses that are likely to be in the flow path of the lahar.

Identifying a special dimension of the self corresponding to one's role as a public scientist does not provide us a magic bullet to resolve every conflict. It is still possible for the lawyer to find that his or her obligations simultaneously move in two or more directions. Likewise, the Earth scientist may find herself bound to act against her own personal preferences. Nor is this meant to imply that the scientist in his or her role as public self speaks from a position of neutrality or objectivity. Quite the contrary, the scientist is acting as an advocate for a specific point of view driven by science. While important, this scientific view has no inherent priority within community debates, in which a variety of other values will come into play. For instance, the community might decide to preserve historic buildings that sit in the path of the lahar, in full knowledge of the likely consequences. But the sense of selfhood described here does allow us to understand advocacy as something other than simply the expression of a personal opinion. It also suggests that such advocacy is, at least at times, intrinsic to the public scientist's work.

In such cases, the public scientist's responsibilities come to resemble those outlined in the codes of ethics of professionals such as engineers. Engineering codes of ethics emphasize that the engineer has a fundamental ethical responsibility to the public that at times supercedes their obligations to their client. It is telling that scientists have been slow to be included within the ranks of professionals such as engineering, the clergy, the military, lawyers, academics, and physicians. We do not need to search far to find the reason for this. The scientific community has sought to avoid the political or ethical commitments that are implied by the notion of the professional. The concepts of professional responsibilities and professional ethics are based upon the distinction of a public from a private self—a distinction whose time has come for the scientific community.

But to accomplish this will require that we revive a more developed notion of the public or political realm and limit the language of economics that has dominated our understanding of the relations between science and society. In recent years, public science agencies have come to recognize the need to address the question of societal relevance. But again, in too many cases this point has been expressed in the language of economics. By speaking of politicians and the public as customers, public scientists have tried to preserve a type of objectivity—or more precisely, subjectivity, in that the public scientist is understood as simply serving the needs of his or her clients. Thus one finds that the USGS Refocused Strategic Plan for 1997–2005 emphasizes the USGS's responsibility to serve its "customers."[15] But the relationship between public science and society is political, not economic. In fact, only the political nature of this relationship—the search for a common good—can save agencies such as the USGS from being eliminated, and their work being farmed out to private concerns.

The public realm is more than a site of electioneering and special interests; it is also the place where we can express ourselves in ways that are impossible through the private pleasures of sentiment or consumerism. But realizing ourselves in this way entails that we reclaim the special dimension of the self exemplified by government science. Scientists today, especially scientists supported by public funds, must see themselves as *political* scientists. If this scrambles established categories, it is no more than what is called for to meet the needs of a new era.

IV.

Following the political and financial shocks of the 1990s, it has become clear that the very existence of public science agencies depends in part upon their skills at being boundary organizations. Boundary organizations serve as buffers and mediators between contrasting interests, translating and interpreting information, values, and perspectives between groups that are often at odds with one another.[16] In the case of the U.S. Geological Survey and the Geological Survey of Canda, these agencies occupy the boundary between society and the environment—Powell's realm of the "geosocial." Indeed, it has even been possible that today these organizations should give as much attention to their responsibilities as boundary organizations as they do to the production of scientific knowledge. Placing Earth science information within meaningful contexts to help us live in a more environmentally benign manner, and learning to treat conversations with the public as dialogues rather than monologues, are two means through which public science can be "translated" into forms people can use.

Such claims still lie at the margins of policy debates within public science agencies. But even if they were generally accepted, we would be left with the question of "skillful means"—how to effectively navigate the boundary between science and society. Recently within the USGS, efforts at linking science to society have focused on the concept of "decision support."[17] The term is a slippery one, and appears in a variety of contexts. Broadly speaking, decision support consists of attempts at managing and disseminating information. Within the field of knowledge management, decision support involves everything from policy to personnel skills to analyzing interactions with the public. Within the artificial intelligence community, decision support focuses on creating expert systems, identifying ways to capture and represent knowledge within a particular domain in order to simulate expertise. Finally, from a software perspective, decision support creates tools that help experts (or in some cases, replace them), through geographical information systems (GIS) and various types of statistical tools.[18]

In its attempts to better serve the public, the USGS is increasingly relying on decision support systems, information tools that use algorithms to produce well-defined answers to complex problems. For instance, the USGS Moist Soil Management Advisor is a software program that helps wildlife refuge managers manage wetlands by calculating what manipulations will control vegetation or salinity problems, and how to properly time floods. Decision support relates science to society primarily by bringing computer technology to bear upon a problem. In the words of one U.S. government publication, "As the decision making process becomes more complex, there will be increasing demands for technology to help decision makers explore and evaluate these issues."[19] In another, the author asks us to imagine county officials, landowners, and citizen groups coming together to discuss a proposed land use development project:

> Using the Internet, the group is able to access much of the needed data to combine with information it has acquired itself . . . they are also able to access the numerical simulation models needed to conduct their analysis, and the visualization software required to display the results.[20]

The author goes on to imagine a resource map "projected on the screen at the front of the assembly or as a holographic image in the center of the room. . . ." "Next, computer model simulations are run depicting potential flood scenarios. . . . A consensus begins to emerge on a land use plan." "In short, the community has built and used a decision support system (DSS) on the fly."[21]

The ruling assumption of such efforts is that decision making is primarily a technical process rather than a political and dialogical one. The bias here is not so much intellectual as informational: it overestimates the usefulness of information in the decision-making process. But rather than more information, or ever more elaborate displays, what people often need most is a chance to speak and the time to mull things over. Coming to understand another's perspective on an issue is often a matter of sympathy rather than technology. In fairness, the decision support literature sometimes recognizes the fact that, in addition to technology, the public also needs a better understanding of science. But there is little appreciation of the fact that decision support is at its heart a political process rather than a technical one; or, for that matter, that the process of education needs to involve the scientist as much as the public.

In other cases, this technical orientation toward relating science to the public gives way to a less quantitative approach. For example, the USGS Volcanic Hazards Program publishes hazard assessments and provides hazards information at a variety of public forums and meetings that it conducts with local and regional officials. In still other instances—as we saw in the virtual reality tour of the Georgia Basin—decision support aims to provide vivid virtual realities for policy makers or the public. Still another approach is that of LUNHA (Land Use History of North America), a series of essays for the nonspecialist that offer a historical context for understanding the ongoing changes in land cover and land use across the North American continent. Similarly, while still in its initial stages, the USGS Marine Realms Information Bank (MRIB) is creating a comprehensive, Web-based geo-library of Earth science information about our coasts and oceans. Developed by the USGS Coastal and Marine Geology Program at Woods Hole, MRIB concerns itself with context rather than content. It focuses upon creating "metadata," that is, information about information that places maps, data files, texts, and pictures within contexts that are attractive and intuitive to a variety of audiences. MRIB's intent is not to create information, but rather to make the information already collected visible to citizens, decision makers, and scientists.[22]

Decision support, then, may be seen as a variety of approaches, ranging from numerical calculations to story lines, intended to provide communities with an overall orientation for discussions. It is not the particular approach that is at issue. Rather, the needs of the audience should drive the choice of approach. In the case of public Earth-science agencies like the GSC and the USGS, the goal is to inform public conversation concerning environmental issues. Given the ecological challenges looming before us, the overall mission of these agencies should be to foster a deep connection between communities and the local and global environments they inhabit. In other words, these agencies can help communities and the nation as a whole write the narratives that will help them chart a path through what is likely to be a challenging future.

Lying at the boundary between society and the environment, public science agencies have a dual mandate: to match a deep commitment to scientific integrity with the goal of furthering democratic decision-making. The public scientist is thus a hybrid creature, scrambling modernist categories of science and politics, uniting within his or her own person categories long thought to be antithetical. To embrace this new role will require both personal and institutional changes. One part of the public scientist's job will continue its traditional role—to research areas that are either outside the nexus of economics, or are too charged with social significance to be privatized. But a sizable part—in principle, half—of the public scientist's responsibilities should be devoted to public communication and dialogue. One corollary of this is that science education must move in two directions—scientists learning about public values as much as informing society about the results of science. This will require that public Earth science agencies integrate their research with skills that are native to the humanities. To fulfill their public charge, public agencies will need to meld environmental justice, epistemology, metaphysics and theology, the perspective of history, and the narrativizing of knowledge with their scientific products.

We inhabit a moral universe; we make sense of experience in terms of intentions, conflicts, and goals. Individuals and cultures cast the events of their lives into a narrative structure in order to understand who they are, to uncover how they came to be the way they are, and to anticipate where they might be going. In everyday life, people depend upon a narrative logic rather than scientific rationality to make sense of their lives. The vast majority of cultural communication—how to fulfill one's role as friend, parent, or sibling, and what counts as laudable behavior or a worthwhile life—has always been expressed through myths and stories. These narratives of personal or societal goals give meaning to the struggle for personal excellence or social justice. These stories also allow us to evaluate the actions of ourselves and others.

We make sense of experience through the logical structure of a narrative. We understand our current situation in terms of our past and possible futures. Narrative logic provides the context of understanding that people need to make sense of facts. When summarizing the findings on global climate change, rather than simply providing a set of contextless numbers (e.g., the prediction of a 1.5°–5° increase in mean global temperature by the year 2100), the scientist can describe a series of possible scenarios or plotlines: more severe storms in the Atlantic, droughts in Colorado, increased crop yields in Siberia, or saltwater intrusion along the coast of Louisiana. By describing these as *possible* scenarios, the scientist acknowledges his or her lack of certainty. But by placing the results of scientific work within a narrative framework, the scientist helps the community grasp the possible implications of its decisions. A narrative can help people make the connection between (for instance) the use of private rather than public transportation, the rise of global temperatures, and the increase in water rates in New Orleans.

By presenting multiple narratives, organizations such as the USGS can explore possible environmental futures without mandating a particular outcome. Scientific information could find its way into public conversation without the patina of modernist certainty. Public scientists would describe a set of likely outcomes that communities could use as they learned to live in an age of limits. The scientist express him- or herself in the language of plausibility rather than calculative certainty, helping communities bring together scientific and political perspectives in order to develop sustainable communities.

The key point is that, in addition to their responsibility to engage in credible, high-quality scientific research, public scientists today are faced with a second professional role: contributing to the creation of both local and planetary narratives. It is a role that cannot be simply farmed out to others, for at least in some cases only the scientist has the nuanced understanding of the issues under consideration. Granted, this second role will not be required of every scientist; a sizable percentage of scientists will continue their research as before. But it has become clear that some fraction of the public science community needs to gain proficiency with expressing the meanings and values that grow out of the research that they know so well.

This is where partnerships with humanists can be helpful. It may be too much to suggest that organizations like the USGS create Offices of Narrative and Values. But there are other ways for public Earth science agencies and the humanities to find common ground. Teams of scientists and humanists can work together on case studies to fashion a common language based in a common set of experiences. Through such experiments, agencies such as the USGS can gain the skills necessary to turn scientific information into social knowledge and political wisdom. In doing so, they may avoid the twin dangers of irrelevance and subjective advocacy, while providing a model of expertise and authority that our culture presently lacks.

9

CONCLUSION

Lay down these words
Before your mind like rocks.
　　　　placed solid, by hands
In choice of place, set
Before the body of the mind
　　　　in space and time:
Solidity of bark, leaf or wall
　　　　riprap of things:
Cobble of milky way,
　　　　straying planets,
These poems, people,
　　　　lost ponies with
Dragging saddles—
　　　　and rocky sure-foot trails.
The worlds like an endless
　　　　four-dimensional
Game of Go.
　　　　ants and pebbles
In the thin loam, each rock a word
　　　　a creek-washed stone
Granite: ingrained
　　　　with torment of fire and weight
Crystal and sediment linked hot
　　　　all change, in thoughts,
As well as things.
　　　　　　　"Riprap" Gary Snyder

Riprap: the inlay of boulders set into the banks of a river, or piled
high as a dam holding back a lake. In a note, Snyder describes riprap

as "a cobble of stone laid on steep slick rock to make a trail for horses in the mountains." For Snyder, it also describes the way thoughts and things fit together: thinking as a process of placing well-dressed stone, and the universe a mosaic too neat to be accidental and too odd to ever be completely comprehended.

Geo-Logic has sought to mark out a common space for the Earth sciences and philosophy. It has framed a mosaic of science, poetry, epistemology, personal experience, metaphysical reflection, and political engagement. Geology has been read as simultaneously scientific and humanistic in nature—the fitted stones of geoscience, geopoetry, geopolitics, and geometaphysics. Fieldwork has been described as a meditative science—a conceptual and toolish riprap constructed from humanistic arts and scientific procedures. Public science agencies have been placed within a border region between science and society, properly responsive to and guiding a patchwork of intersecting groups, perspectives, and interests. Addressing these varied publics requires rhetorical nuance and narrative skill as well as logical acumen. Altogether, the sciences and the humanities have been portrayed as the joint links between society and nature, connecting much more than two things, since neither society nor nature is a single entity.

Scott McLean, Eldridge Moores, and David Robertson argue that scientific advances do not truly become the possession of a culture until these discoveries are expressed through that culture's art and poetry.[1] They interpret Snyder as serving a role for 20th century geology similar to John Donne's for 17th century astronomy. Just as Donne expressed the existential consequences of the Copernican revolution, Snyder helps us understand the implications of recent revolutions in our understanding of the Earth.[2] Snyder's poems render deep time into our own time, finding the pulse of shifting plates within rigid strata warped by overwhelming pressures. Snyder gives words to the meanings implicit within limestone and gneiss, where space is shown to be the inscription of time upon reality:

> ten million years ago an ocean floor
> glides like a snake beneath the continent crunching up
> old seabed till it's high as alps.[3]

But there are also other ways to explore the new space that geology inhabits. One example is "Real World Experiments," a program launched in the spring of 2002 at the University of Bielefeld in Germany. Directed by Matthias Gros and Holger Hoffmann-Riem at

Bielefeld's Institute for Science and Technology Studies (IWT), real-world experiments are attempts to solve environmental problems under uncontrolled or "field" conditions. "Experiment" is understood here as a process of iterative self-experimentation involving both nature and society—an approach that is in stark contrast to the isolated terms of the laboratory experiment. "Real World Experiments" is focusing on a set of case studies of human intervention in ecological systems, including dune restoration, landscape design, lake restoration, and waste management. The overall aim of the program is to develop intellectual tools "for the planning and implementation of scientifically reliable and socially robust approaches of environmental design"[4] (GL:CH9).

A second, similar effort underway is "New Directions in the Earth Sciences and the Humanities." New Directions was launched in the spring of 2001 with an initial grant from the Colorado School of Mines. It has subsequently received support from the NSF, NASA, the USGS, the EPA, the National Endowment for the Humanities, the National Center for Atmospheric Research, and the Geological Survey of Canada, as well as a consortium of universities (numbering eleven to date). The work of New Directions turns on three questions: What can the humanities contribute to environmental solutions? How can we make scientific information more pertinent to society? And, what is the future of knowledge? (GL:CH9).

In addition to a number of workshops and conferences, New Directions has provided initial funding for seven interdisciplinary case studies. These case studies are run by teams consisting of at least one scientist and one humanist. For instance, in the project "Humanizing Environmental Research on the South Carolina Coast," a marine biologist and a philosopher work with students to link scientific data to the needs of local communities. In "Ecology and Cultural History of the Neva River, St. Petersburg, Russia," experts in Russian literature, landscape architecture, and geology examine the relation between the Neva River's ecological problems and its iconic status in Russian history and literature. The upshot of these efforts will include improving the usefulness of public science, creating new venues for citizen and stakeholder participation in environmental decision making, gaining greater understanding in how to conduct interdisciplinary research and dialogue, and how to more richly express the human dimensions of our relationship with the environment.[5]

Another attempt at integrating the sciences and the humanities—also concerned with the problem of acid mine drainage—is "AMD&ART." Drainage from abandoned coal mines is a widespread environmental problem in Pennsylvania and Appalachia, with significant regional economic and social impacts. AMD&ART is working to amend the negative attitudes toward and within this region through the creation of large-scale public places that address the problems of acid drainage from scientific and artistic points of view. In existence since 1994, AMD&ART combines these different perspectives with the engagement of local communities for the design of "interpretive trails will draw together historical information, the science behind passive AMD treatment, and the newly healed ecosystem that will thrive in the wake of remediation." Working with a number of partners at three sites in Southwestern Pennsylvania, AMD&ART is attempting to prove that such as approach can succeed on both the watershed and regional scale[6] (GL:CH9).

A final example is worth noting, one that is operating on the K-12 level. The Flatirons Outdoor Classroom is a project within the Boulder Valley School District in Boulder, Colorado, that consists of an interdisciplinary outdoor learning environment combining elements of science, art, social studies, and the humanities. The project has two parts. Phase 1 (now largely completed) focused on the creation of an integrated outdoor classroom space. Phase 2 proposes the development of curriculum projects to make full use of this unique space.

The classroom itself consists of four elements. A riverbed runs the length of the school building (135 feet), offering a depiction of the Boulder Creek watershed. At the top, students are able to fill a 600 gallon reservoir with water, and then send a flood down the channel. Streamflows are used for experiments in hydrology and sedimentology, as well as for thought experiments in water politics (e.g., learning about senior/junior water rights and the possible effects of 100 year floods along Boulder Creek). The water is captured in a large underground cistern, and pumped back up to the reservoir for repeated experiments. Second, a geology exhibit uses samples of local strata to represent the Flatirons and other regional features of the Rocky Mountains and High Plains. Adjacent to the rocks, on the side of the building, a large mural is being created that depicts Colorado across geologic history. Utilizing reproductions of paintings commissioned by the Denver Museum of Nature and Science—a partner on the project—teachers will be able to move back and forth between the representations of ancient Denver and the rock outcrops, instructing students in the nature of scientific research by juxtaposing the geologic strata to pictures of the geologic past.

Third, a performing arts area sits adjacent to the geology exhibit, consisting of a stage and a terraced seating area, with the streambed running between. A small Zen garden also rests between the geology exhibits and the stage, providing opportunities for artistic expression and personal development. Finally, on the eastern end of the project a botanical garden has been created: in addition to various types of garden plants, the space will be used for cultivating plants used by Western pioneers. Students in each grade level will have direct curricular ties to the classroom: studying water, rock, and the soil; planting seeds, bulbs and vegetable crops; watching and learning about insects and birds; and caring for the Zen garden (GL: CH9). Teachers will use each of these areas as teaching tools to explore the connections between scientific investigations and artistic expression.

Phase 2 plans—just launched—call for the dissemination of the curricular ideas generated by the outdoor classroom. After a series of in-services where district teachers will receive training in integrating the earth sciences and the humanities within the classroom space, regional workshops will be run at the outdoor classroom, where educators can use this site as the model for research and discussion of interdisciplinary approaches to K-12 education. The goal is to create a model that will help schools nationwide apply the principles learned here for developing interdisciplinary outdoor classrooms in their own localities nationwide (GL:CH9)

All of these projects are at a fairly early stage in their development, and so their ultimate success or failure remains a question for the future. But they are also represent novel attempts to revitalize public discourse and environmental education through the integration of the humanities with our societal concerns. In fairness, it is to be expected that it will take a number of years to gauge the true measure of the success of these projects. For if we are on the cusp of an era that is truly named post-modern, in search of genuinely new models of thinking, education, and institutional expression, then it makes sense to view these efforts as the first halting steps of an extended cultural experiment. After all, it took modernity two hundred years to make good on the promise of its approach. We cannot write these and similar efforts a blank check, if for no other reason than the exigencies of funding agencies demand deliverables on a clear schedule. But we may nonetheless view the projects described here, and argued for throughout this work, on a timeline that partakes of the geological.

NOTES

Preface

1. Information on *Global Climate Change and Society* can be found at http://sciencepolicy.colorado.edu/gccs.

2. *Earth Matters: The Earth Sciences, Philosophy, and the Claims of Community,* ed. Robert Frodeman, (Englewood Cliffs, N.J.: Prentice-Hall), 2000.

Chapter 1. Introduction

1. Cf. Jürgen Habermas, *The Structural Transformation of the Public Sphere,* trans. Thomas Burger. (Cambridge: MIT Press, 1989).

2. Readers will find ambiguities in my use of "geology"—referring at times to lithology, the integrated study of the Earth, and finally to a full-bodied *logos* of Gaia that integrates the humanities. I trust that context will be sufficient to distinguish which meaning is primary. It is also worth noting that my use of "Gaia" implies no attachment to Lovelock's "Gaia Hypothesis." For Lovelock's views, *The Ages of Gaia: A Biography of our Living Earth* (New York: Norton, 1988).

3. On the former point, see Paul Shepard, *Nature and Madness* (San Francisco: Sierra Club Books, 1982), and David Abram, *The Spell of the Sensuous* (New York: Pantheon, 1996).

4.Kai N. Lee, *Compass and Gyroscope: Integrating Science and Politics for the Environment* (Washington, D.C.: Island Press, 1993).

5. There is no accepted definition of which disciplines constitute the humanities. I will use the term to include philosophy, literature, foreign languages, history, theology or religious studies, art history, and the nonquantitatively oriented parts of the social sciences. Cf. Robert E. Proctor, *Defining the Humanities* (Bloomington: Indiana University Press, 1998).

6. This assertion will draw fire. And certainly values are debatable: that is the function of democratic debate. But, to take two simple examples: few would argue with the claim that open-mindedness is better than dogmatism, or that pluralism is preferable to bigotry.

7. Stephen J. Pyne, *How the Canyon Became Grand* (New York: Penguin Books, 1998).

8. Immanuel Kant, *Grounding for the Metaphysics of Morals*, trans. James W. Ellington (Indianapolis: Hackett Publishing, 1981), p. 2.

9. It is worth noting that our standard for what counts as a competent degree of expertise is as much a social, political, economic, and technological question as it is an epistemological one: standards of sufficient expertise change as society's interests change, more money is invested, and technology advances.

10. Ralph Waldo Emerson, "The American Scholar," in *Selections from Ralph Waldo Emerson*, ed. Stephen E. Whicher (Boston: Houghton Mifflin, 1960), p. 70.

11. *Zen and the Ways*, trans. and ed. Trevor Leggett (Boston: Routledge and Kegan Paul, 1978), p. 221.

12. Not a nuclear explosion, but rather a hydrothermal explosion when water comes in contact with hot nuclear waste, potentially spreading radionuclides throughout the water table.

13. E.g., Alphonso Lingis, *Excesses: Eros and Culture* (Albany: SUNY Press, 1984); *Abuses* (Berkeley: University of California Press, 1994), and *The Community of Those Who Have Nothing in Common* (Bloomington: University of Indiana Press, 1994).

14. Recent years have seen another dustup around the question of evolution involving mathematicians and physicists versus biologists and paleontologists. "Is biology too difficult for biologists?" begins a 1998 book review in *Nature* written by Per Bok, a physicist who claims that the mathematics of complexity theory can account for the mass extinctions found in the fossil record. See Richard Monastersky, "Fossils vs. the Formula," *Chronicle of Higher Education*, 47, no. 35 (11 May 2001): A16–A18.

15. On the emergence of geology out of mineralogy, see Rachel Laudan, *From Mineralogy to Geology: The Foundations of a Science, 1650–1830* (Chicago: University of Chicago Press, 1987).

16. One sign of this transitional status is the recent National Academy of Science report: Committee on Future Roles, Challenges, and Opportunities for the U.S. Geological Survey, *Future Roles and Opportunities for the U.S. Geological Survey* (Washington, D.C.: National Research Council, 2001).

Chapter 2. Acid Mine Philosophy

1. On Hegel's dialectic, see e.g., Stanley Rosen, *G. F. W. Hegel: An Introduction to the Science of Wisdom* (New Haven: Yale University Press), 1974.

2. For instance, in Spain in April 1998 a mine tailings pond failed, releasing zinc, lead, and cadmium along a twenty-mile section of the Guadiamar River. The accident contaminated the aquifer connected to the Donana wildlife reserve, and destroyed six thousand hectares of farmland.

3. Cf. Carlos D. Da Rosa and James S., Lyon. *Golden Dreams, Poisoned Streams* (Washington, D.C.: Mineral Policy Center, 1997), p. 13. In 1996, the U.S. General Accounting Office assessed the impacts of mining to include five thousand miles of impacted streams, 50 billion tons of mine waste, and fourteen thousand sites in need of serious remediation.

4. "Navigable" is here meant in the common, rather than the technical, sense of the Clean Water Act (see below).

5. For an account of the Summitville site, see Geoffrey S. Plumlee, *The Summitville Mine and its Downstream Effects*: An on-line update of Open File Report 95-23. Available at http://greenwood.cr.usgs.gov/pub/open-file-reports/ofr-95-0023/summit.htm.

6. John Marshall and Zeke Zanoni, *Mining the Hard Rock in the San Juans* (Silverton, Colo.: Simpler Way Press, 1996), p. 24.

7. See Olga L. Moya and Andrew L. Fono, *Federal Environmental Law: The User's Guide* (St. Paul, Minn.: West Publishing, 1997), p. 288.

8. Under the Clean Water Act, navigable is defined as including almost any body of water (with the exception of groundwater), including potholes, intermittent streams, dry washes, canals, and wetlands.

9. Moya and Fono. *Federal Environmental Law,* p. 289; Clean Water Act Section 101, 33 U.S.C. ⸹1251 (1972).

10. In at least some areas (e.g., EPA Region VIII, covering the Rocky Mountains) the EPA has exercised its authority more subtly over time. Region VIII strives to work with states on the front-end of rule-makings, rather than just rejecting them months or years later.

11. "Animas Status Report," *Colorado Center for Environmental Management,* May 1996.

12. Interviews with Chris Hayes, attorney for Sunnyside Gold Corporation, 11 February 1999, and Carol Russell, EPA official, Region VIII, 16 February 1999.

13. Interview with Chris Hayes.

14. These included the possibility that efflorescent salts that formed during mining could lead to the continued production of acidic waters even after flooding, and the difficulty of completely flooding the mine due to myriad fractures and seasonal variations. Kirk Nordstrom, U.S. Geological Survey, personal communication, 15 April 1999.

15. Interview with Larry Perino, Sunnyside Gold Corporation, 12 April 1999.

16. W. G. Wright, "Natural and Mining-Related Sources of Dissolved Minerals during Low Flow in the Upper Animas River Basin," Southwestern Colorado, USGS Fact Sheet FS 148-97, October 1997.

17. Michael Polanyi, *Personal Knowledge: Towards a Post-Critical Philosophy* (New York: Harper & Row, 1964), 428 p.

18. "In this alternating determination of the finite and the infinite from one to the other and back again, their truth is already implicitly present, and all that is required is to take up what is before us." *Hegel's Science of Logic*, trans. A.V. Miller (New York: Humanities Press, 1976), p. 143.

Chapter 3. Corrosive Effects

1. Cf. Carolyn Merchant, *The Death of Nature* (New York: Harper Collins, 1980), p. 32.

2. The city of Durango did attempt to sue the Gold King Mine and San Juan County for contaminating their water source in 1906. Today Durango's drinking water comes from another watershed, that of the Florida River.

3. Personal communications with Durango District office, Colorado Water Quality Control Division, Colorado Division of Public Health and Environment, 2 April 1999.

4. Daniel Sarewitz, "Science and Environmental Policy: An Excess of Objectivity," in *Earth Matters: The Earth Sciences and Contemporary Culture*, ed. Robert Frodeman (Upper Saddle River, N.J.: Prentice-Hall, 2000).

5. For a recent account of the controversy, see Charles C. Mann, and Mark L. Plummer, "Can Science Rescue Salmon?" *Science* 289 (4 August 2000): 716–19.

6. Joseph Taylor III, quoted in ibid., p. 717.

7. While a phenomenologically oriented environmental metaphysics or theology is yet to be written, environmental religion has been addressed by a number of authors, including Max Oelschlaeger, *Caring for Creation: An Ecumenical Approach to the Environmental Crisis* (New Haven: Yale University Press, 1994); Dolores LaChapelle, *Sacred Land, Sacred Sex* (Silverton, Colo: Finn Hill Arts, 1988); and Eugene Hargrove, ed., *Religion and Environmental Crisis* (Athens: University of Georgia Press, 1986).

8. One could certainly chart other routes through this territory—for instance, through an account of the work of Arne Naess or John Passmore.

9. More precisely, this caused philosophers such as Nietzsche to try to redefine human purpose as self-created.

10. See, for instance, Eric Katz, *Nature as Subject: Human Obligation and Natural Community* (Lanham, Md.: Rowman & Littlefield, 1996); and Max Oelschlaeger, *The Idea of Wilderness: From Prehistory to the Age of Ecology* (New Haven: Yale University Press, 1993).

11. See Bill McKibben, *The End of Nature* (New York: Random House, 1989); and William Cronin, "The Trouble with Nature," in *Uncommon Ground: Rethinking the Human Place in Nature* (New York: W.W. Norton, 1995).

12. Katz, *Nature as Subject*.

13. Bruce V. Foltz, *Inhabiting the Earth: Heidegger, Environmental Ethics, and the Metaphysics of Nature* (Atlantic Highlands, N.J.: Humanities Press, 1995).

14. One prominent source for discussion of this sort is the journal *Restoration and Management Notes* (now called *Ecological Restoration, North America*).

15. http://www.nae.edu/nae/naehome.nsf/weblinks/NAEW-4NHMD8?opendocument. See also http://www.cc.jyu.fi/helsie/pdf/allenby.pdf).

16. Brad Allenby, "Earth Systems Engineering and Management," *IEEE Technology and Society Magazine,* winter, 2000/2001, p. 21. It is worth noting that some philosophers have come to essentially the same conclusion: see Steven Vogel, "Environmental Philosophy after the End of Nature," *Environmental Ethics,* vol. 24, Spring 2002, pp. 23–39.

17. Chris Maser, "Ends and Means: Restoration and the Future of Land Management," *Restoration and Management Notes* 6 (1988): 29; quoted in Mark Cowell, "Ecological Restoration and Environmental Ethics," *Environmental Ethics* 15, no. 1 (spring 1993): 19–32.

18. Carolyn Merchant, "Restoration and Reunion with Nature," *Restoration and Management Notes* 4 (1986); Andrew Light, "Restoration, the Value of Participation, and the Risks of Professionalization," in *Restoring Nature: Perspectives from the Social Sciences and the Humanities,* ed. Paul H. Gobster and R. Bruce Hull (Washington, D.C.: Island Press, 2000).

19. Françoise d'Eaubonne, *Le Féminisme ou la mort* (Paris: Pierre Horay, 1974). I am indebted to Trish Glazebrook for much of the following account of ecofeminism. See her "Heidegger and Ecofeminism," in *Re-Reading the Canon: Feminist Interpretations of Heidegger,* ed. Nancy Holland and Patricia Huntington (University Park: The Pennsylvania State University Press, 2001).

20. Rosemary Radford Ruether, *New Woman/New Earth: Sexist Ideologies and Human Liberation* (New York: Seabury Press, 1975), 204.

21. See, for instance, Paula Gunn Allen, *The Sacred Hoop: Recovering the Feminine in American Indian Tradition* (Boston: Beacon Press, 1986); and *Healing the Wounds: The Promise of Ecofeminism,* ed. Judith Plant (Santa Cruz, Calif.: New Society Publishers, 1989).

22. Chris Cuomo, "Toward Thoughtful Ecofeminist Activism," in *Ecological Feminist Perspectives,* ed. Karen J. Warren (Bloomington: Indiana University Press, 1996), 42–51; Stephanie Lahar, "Ecofeminist Theory and Grassroots Politics," *Hypatia* 6, no. 1 (1991): 28–45.

23. The term belongs in quotation marks to highlight the question of whether "pollution" only applies to human activity. Can a naturally occurring chemical count as pollution?

24. Robert Elliott, "Faking Nature," *Inquiry* 25, no. 1 (March 1982): 81–93. Expanded into *Faking Nature: The Ethics of Environmental Restoration* (Lanham, Md.: Rowman and Littlefield, 1997).

25. Many will doubt that it is possible to fully restore an ecosystem or the natural features of the land. But to argue on these grounds is to make the preservation of nature dependent upon technological insufficiency. If—or better said, given the speed of technological advance, *when*—we are able to reconstruct ecosystems, this objection becomes irrelevant.

26. Andrew Light observes that a restored landscape might better be compared to a restored work of art, rather than a faked one. Andrew Light, "Ecological Restoration and the Culture of Nature: A Pragmatic Perspective," in Gobster and Hull, *Restoring Nature*.

27. Paul Ricoeur, *The Symbolism of Evil* (New York: Harper and Row, 1967), 33.

28. For the former claim, see Al Gore, *Earth in the Balance: Ecology and the Human Spirit* (New York: Houghton Mifflin, 1993); Theodore Roszak, *The Voice of the Earth* (New York: Simon & Schuster, 1992).

29. Mircea Eliade, *The Sacred and the Profane*, trans. Willard Trask (New York: Harcourt Brace, 1968), p. 10. Italics in the original.

30. "The sacred tree, the sacred stone are not adored as stone or tree; they are worshipped precisely because they are *hierophanies*, because they show something that is no longer stone or tree but the *sacred*, the *ganz andere* [wholly other]." Ibid., 12. Italics in the original.

31. "Man first reads the sacred on the world, on some elements or aspects of the world, on the heavens, on the sun and moon, on the waters and vegetation." Ricoeur, *Symbolism of Evil*, p. 10.

32. "A wilderness, in contrast with those areas where man and his own works dominate the landscape, is hereby recognized as an area where the earth and its community of life are untrammeled by man, where man himself is a visitor who does not remain. An area of wilderness is further defined to mean in this Act an area of undeveloped Federal land retaining its primeval character and influence, without permanent improvements or human habitation, which is protected and managed so as to preserve its natural conditions and which (1) generally appears to have been affected primarily by the forces of nature, with the imprint of man's work substantially unnoticeable. . . ." Public Law 88-577, 88th Congress, S. 4, 3 September 1964.

33. Two recent examples are the 2001 annual meeting of the International Association for Environmental Philosophy, which sponsored a day-long meeting with the title "Nature and the Sacred," and the Lilly Fellows National Research Conference entitled "Ecology, Theology, and Judeo-Christian Environmental Ethics," held at Notre Dame University on 21–24 February 2002.

Chapter 4. The Places of Science

1. Friedrich Nietzsche, *The Gay Science*, trans. Walter Kaufmann (New York: Random House, 1974), #125.

2. Two recent summaries of the debate are *Science Wars*, ed. Andrew Ross (London: Duke University Press, 1996), and *Beyond the Science Wars*, ed. Ullica Segerstrala (Albany: SUNY Press, 2000). Steve Fuller founded a journal, *Social Epistemology*, devoted to the question of societal effects of epistemological stances.

3. A space inhabited by, among others, Ian Hacking, *Representing and Intervening* (New York: Cambridge University Press, 1983); Nancy Cartwright, *The Dappled World: A Study of the Boundaries of Science* (New York: Cambridge University Press, 1999); Trish Glazebrook, *Heidegger's Philosophy of Science* (New York: Fordham University Press, 2000); and Ronald N. Giere, *Science without Laws* (Chicago: University of Chicago Press, 1999).

4. Giere, *Science without Laws*, p. 4.

5. Cartwright, *Dappled World*, p. 1.

6. Other possibilities include viewing the philosophy of science as a branch of the philosophy of technology, or as a subdivision of the philosophy of religion.

7. Jacques Derrida, *Margins of Philosophy*, trans. Alan Bass (Chicago: University of Chicago Press, 1982).

8. See, for instance, George Lakoff and Mark Johnson, *Philosophy in the Flesh: The Embodied Mind and Its Challenge to Western Thought* (New York: Basic Books, 1999); and Marvin Minsky, *The Society of Mind* (New York: Simon & Schuster, 1986).

9. "The ability to perceive similarities and analogies is one of the most fundamental aspects of human cognition." Stella Vosniadou and Andrew Ortony, *Similarity and Analogical Reasoning* (Cambridge: Cambridge University Press, 1989), p. 1.

10. Nancy Cartwright, *How the Laws of Physics Lie* (Oxford: Clarendon Press, 1983).

11. Even this assumption is not strictly correct: for example, Coriolis forces differ in these places.

12. The literature on analogy in science includes Mary B. Hesse, *Models and Analogies in Science* (Notre Dame, Ind.: University of Notre Dame Press, 1966).

13. Other popular textbooks in the philosophy of science take the same approach: for instance, the table of contents of the third edition of Alan F. Chalmer's *What Is This Thing Called Science* (New York: Heckett, 1999) runs as follows. 1. Science and Knowledge Derived from the Facts of Experience. 2. Observation as Practical Intervention 3. Experiment. 4. Deriving Facts from Theories. 5. Introducing Falsificationism. 6. Sophisticated Falsificationism: Novel Predictions and the Growth of Knowledge. 7. The Limitations of Falsificationism. 8. Theories as Structures I: Kuhn's Paradigms. 9. Theories as

Structures II: Research Programs. 10. Feyerabend's Anarchistic Theory of Science. 11. Methodical Changes in Method. 12. The Bayesian Approach. 13. The New Experimentalism. 14. Why Should the World Obey Laws? 15. Realism and Antirealism. (Such examples can be multiplied).

14. Steve Fuller has argued along similar lines: see *Social Epistemology* (Bloomington: Indiana University Press, 2002).

15. Maurice Merleau-Ponty, *The Phenomenology of Perception* (London: Routledge & Kegan Paul, 1962).

16. These points are further developed in Thomas Raab and Robert Frodeman, "What Is It Like to Be a Geologist? The Phenomenology of Geology and Its Implications," *Philosophy and Geography*, July 2002.

17. Hubert L. Dreyfus and Stuart E. Dreyfus. *Mind over Machine: The Power of Human Intuition and Expertise in the Era of the Computer* (New York: Free Press, 1986).

18. Naomi Oreskes. "Why Believe a Computer? Models, Measures, and Meaning in the Natural World," in *The Earth Around Us: Maintaining a Livable Planet*, ed. Jill S. Schneiderman (New York: W. H. Freeman, 2000).

19. John Harte, *Consider a Spherical Cow: A Course in Environmental Problem Solving* (Los Altos, Calif.: W. Kaufmann, 1985).

20. Cf. Victor R. Baker, "Conversing with the Earth: The Geological Approach to Understanding," in *Earth Matters: The Earth Sciences and Contemporary Culture*, ed. Robert Frodeman (Upper Saddle River, N.J.: Prentice-Hall, 2000).

21. Starlink, the creation of AgrEvo, Inc., is a type of corn genetically modified with a gene from a bacterium that kills worms that eat corn. The EPA, concerned that Starlink could cause allergic reactions, approved corn for animal feed, but not for human consumption. AgrEvo signed an agreement that it would oversee the distribution of the seed so that it would not get mixed with corn for humans. The company claimed it had a set of procedures to ensure the two would be kept separate—e.g., a 660-foot buffer around fields of Starlink. But Starlink was discovered in taco shells in October 2001 leading to a nationwide recall of this and other products containing the corn. This affected farmers nationwide).

Chapter 5. Earth Stories

1. See Rachel Lauden, *From Mineralogy to Geology: The Foundations of a Science, 1650–1830* (Chicago: University of Chicago Press, 1987).

2. Possibly the most humanistic treatment of geology is contained in the writings of John McPhee. See, for instance, *Basin and Range* (New York: Farrar, Straus and Giroux, 1981), *In Suspect Terrain* (New York: Farrar, Straus and Giroux, 1983), and *Assembling California* (New York: Farrar, Straus and Giroux, 1993).

3. See Nelson Goodman, "Uniformity and Simplicity," in *Uniformity and Simplicity: A Symposium on the Principle of the Uniformity of Nature*, ed. C. C. Albritton Jr. et al., Special Paper (New York: Geological Society of America, 1967), 99; and Richard Watson, "Explanation and Prediction in Geology," *Journal of Geology* 77 (1969): 488. Although not concerned with the question of the status of geology as a science, John Sallis's *Stone* (Bloomington: Indiana University Press, 1994), is a recent exception to the general neglect of geology by philosophers.

4. R. N. Giere. *Explaining Science: A Cognitive Approach* (Chicago: University of Chicago Press, 1988); N. Oreskes, K. S. Shrader-Frechette, and K. Belitz, "Verification, Validation, and Confirmation of Numerical Models in the Earth Sciences," *Science* 263 (1994): 641–46.

5. Kristen Shrader-Frechette, *Burying Uncertainty: Risk and the Case against Geological Disposal of Nuclear Waste* (Berkeley: University of California Press, 1993).

6. David B. Kitts, *The Structure of Geology* (Dallas, Tex.: SMU Press, 1977); W. V. Engelhardt and J. Zimmermann, *Theory of Earth Science* (1982; reprint, New York: Cambridge University Press, 1988).

7. For accounts on the latter, see Alexander Koyre, *From the Closed World to the Infinite Universe* (Baltimore: Johns Hopkins University Press, 1957); and Thomas Kuhn, *The Copernican Revolution: Planetary Astronomy in the Development of Western Thought* (Cambridge: Harvard University Press, 1957). "Deep time" was coined by John McPhee: cf. *Basin and Range*.

8. Since Hegel, time has been a central issue within Continental philosophy. One measure of this is Heidegger's *Being and Time*, the twentieth century's most influential work in Continental philosophy. But despite the prominence of historicist approaches within contemporary Continental philosophy, geologic time has gotten no attention. The cultural implications of geologic time are more typical of the history of ideas than of philosophy: see Charles Gillispie, *Genesis and Geology* (New York: Harper, 1959); Stephen Toulmin and June Goodfield, *The Discovery of Time* (New York: Harper & Row, 1965); and Stephen Goldman, "Modern Science and Western Culture: The Issue of Time," *History of European Ideas* 3, no. 4 (1982): 371–401.

9. "I met a traveller from an antique land
   Who said: Two vast and trunkless legs of stone
   Stand in the desert. Near them, on the sand,
   Half sunk, a shattered visage lies, whose frown,
   And wrinkled lip, and sneer of cold command,
   Tell that its sculptor well those passions read
   Which yet survive, stamped on these lifeless things,
   The hand that mocked them, and the heart that fed;
   And on the pedestal these words appear:
   "My name is Ozymandias, king of kings:
   Look on my works, ye Mighty, and despair!"
   Nothing beside remains. Round the decay

Of that colossal wreck, boundless and bare
The lone and level sands stretch far away."
                              —Percy Bysshe Shelley (1818)

10. My account here is a gloss upon a story that is quite complex. One might well reply that today, when the philosophy of science considers physics the paradigmatic science, it has in mind physics qua relativity theory and quantum mechanics rather than classical mechanics. My point turns upon distinguishing between the state of knowledge *within* a given field and the representation of that field *outside* the realm of specialists. Possibly the most remarkable thing about the new physics is how little impact it has had upon our culture's general epistemological views, whether within the intellectual community or the public at large. Physics qua classical mechanics still provides us with our basic model for understanding the nature of knowledge. Consider, for instance, how introductory physics is taught in American colleges—typically beginning with several weeks on classical mechanics. Quantum mechanics is not taught until the third semester of physics, well after the vast majority of students have stopped taking physics. While physicists struggle to integrate quantum physics into an overall picture of reality, classical mechanics still provides the pedagogical model for understanding the nature of science, and indeed of knowledge in general.

11. For the classic statement of this claim, cf. Descartes's *Rules for the Direction of the Mind,* trans. with an introduction by Laurence J. Lafleur (Indianapolis: Liberal Arts Press; written in 1627 and first published in 1701).

12. See G. K. Gilbert, "The Inculcation of Scientific Method by Example," *American Journal of Science,* 3d ser., 31 (1886): 284–99; and T. C. Chamberlin, "The Method of Multiple Working Hypotheses," *Science* 15 (1890): 92–96.

13. See, for instance, Claude Albritton, *The Fabric of Geology* (Reading, Mass: Addison-Wesley, 1963); Stanley A. Schumm, *To Interpret the Earth* (New York: Cambridge University Press, 1991); and Derek V. Ager, *The Nature of the Stratigraphical Record* (Chichester, NY: J. Wiley 1993).

14. Stephen Jay Gould, *Time's Arrow, Time's Cycle* (Cambridge: Harvard University Press, 1987), and *Wonderful Life* (New York: W. W. Norton, 1989); Peter D. Ward, *Time Machines: Scientific Explorations in Deep Time* (New York: Copernicus, 1998); Niles Eldredge, *Dominion* (New York: H. Holt, 1995); and Edward O. Wilson, *Consilience: The Unity of Knowledge* (New York: Knopf, 1998). Gould's *Wonderful Life,* pp. 277–91, is especially relevant to the points I will be making.

15. Doreen Massey, "Space-Time, Science, and the Relationship between Physical Geography and Human Geography," *Institute of British Geography* 24 (1999): 264.

16. Schumm, *To Intrepret the Earth,* p. 5.

17. See Alan Sokal, "Transgressing the Boundaries: Toward a Transformative Hermeneutics of Quantum Gravity," *Social Text,* nos. 46/47 (spring/summer 1996): 217–52, also available at http://www.physics.nyu.edu/faculty/sokal/.
   What follows summarizes a complex and controversial history. Its complexity derives partly from the fact that we are simultaneously considering discussions by philoso-

phers of science, along with the impact of these discussions upon those within the scientific community. For other accounts see Ian Hacking, *Representing and Intervening* (New York: Cambridge University Press, 1983); John Rajchman and Cornel West, *Post-Analytic Philosophy* (New York: Columbia University Press, 1985); Richard Rorty, *Philosophy and the Mirror of Nature* (Princeton: Princeton University Press, 1979); Ronald Giere, *Explaining Science* (Chicago: University of Chicago Press, 1988); Joseph Rouse, *Knowledge and Power* (Ithaca: Cornell University Press, 1987); and Philip Kitcher, *The Advancement of Science* (New York: Oxford University Press, 1993). It should be emphasized that the new view of science that I argue for in terms of Continental philosophy, could also, with some modifications, be made in terms of recent analytic philosophy of science.

18. Feyerabend was an important early exception to the belief in the scientific method's unity. Paul Feyerabend, "Problems of Empiricism," in *Beyond the Edge of Certainty*, ed. R. Colodny (Englewood Cliffs, N.J.: Prentice-Hall, 1965).

19. This positivist orientation remains important within analytic philosophy of science. Recent work in the fields of cognitive science, artificial intelligence, and evolutionary epistemology still shares these general assumptions. See H. Kornblith, ed., *Naturalizing Epistemology* (Cambridge: MIT Press, 1985); Paul M. Churchland, *Matter and Consciousness* (Cambridge: MIT Press, 1988); and Paul Thagard, *Conceptual Revolutions* (Princeton: Princeton University Press, 1992).

20. While Kuhn's work was the single most important impetus for the changes that I will discuss, he is a symbolic figure representing a larger movement within the philosophy of science. Other important authors include Toulmin and Goodfield, Hanson, and Feyerabend.

21. This is a "strong" interpretation of Kuhn's work. Kuhn himself vacillated on the degree to which the results of science are shaped by social values. In his later essays (e.g., *The Essential Tension* [Chicago: University of Chicago Press, 1977]), he retreated from some of the claims made in *The Structure of Scientific Revolutions*. This has not stopped others from following the earlier, more radical Kuhn. Joseph Rouse speaks of there being two Kuhns, one more radical, the other more conventional in his attitudes.

22. Exceptions to the general neglect of the philosophy of science by Continental philosophy include Patrick A. Heelan, *Space-Perception and the Philosophy of Science* (Berkeley: University of California Press, 1983); Joseph J. Kockelmans and Theodore J. Kisiel, eds., *Phenomenology and the Natural Sciences: Essays and Translations* (Evanston, Ill.: Northwestern University Press, 1970); Joseph Rouse, *Engaging Science: How to Understand its Practices Philosophically* (Ithaca: Cornell University Press, 1996); Babette E. Babich et al., eds., *Continental and Postmodern Perspectives in the Philosophy of Science* (Brookfield, Vt.: Avebury Press, 1995); and Glazebrook, *Heidegger's Philosophy of Science*.

23. For an introductory text in hermeneutics, see Josef Bleicher, *Contemporary Hermeneutics* (Boston: Routledge & Kegan Paul, 1980). Hans-Georg Gadamer's *Truth and Method* (New York: Seabury Press, 1975) offers a more sophisticated historical account.

172 *Notes*

24. For a recent account of Heidegger's views on natural science, see Glazebrook, *Heidegger's Philosophy of Science.*

25. On the visual nature of the science of geology, see Martin J. S. Rudwick, "The Emergence of a Visual Language for Geological Science, 1760–1840," *History of Science* (1976): 149–95.

26. Maurice Merleau-Ponty, "Eye and Mind," in *The Merleau-Ponty Aesthetics Reader*, ed. Galen A. Johnson, trans. Michael B. Smith (Evanston, Ill.: Northwestern University Press, 1993).

27. Sokal comments, in the essay where he revealed his hoax, that anyone who believes the laws of physics to be mere conventions "is invited to try transgressing those conventions from the windows of my apartment. (I live on the twenty-first floor.)" His example, however, is telling. Socially relevant science, like questions of acid mine drainage and global climate change, defy simplistic accounts of scientific objectivity. See Alan Sokal, "A Physicist Experiments with Cultural Studies," *Lingua Franca*, May/June 1996, pp. 62–64.

28. The following argument, dependent upon an entire tradition of hermeneutic philosophy, relies upon Heidegger's *Being and Time,* trans. John MacQuarrie and Edward Robinson (London: SCM Press, 1962), originally published in German in 1927.

29. Work on the social and political influences upon scientific research include Bruno Latour and Steven Woolgar, *Laboratory Life: The Social Construction of Scientific Fact* (Beverly Hills, Calif.: Sage Publications, 1979); Andrew Pickering, ed., *Science as Practice and Culture* (Chicago: University of Chicago Press, 1992); Sharon Traweek, *Beamtimes and Lifetimes* (Cambridge: Harvard University Press, 1988); and Karin Knorr-Cetina, *Epistemic Cultures: How the Sciences Make Knowledge* (Cambridge: Harvard University Press, 1999).

30. Harry M. Collins and Trevor Pinch have described the extraordinary difficulties scientists sometimes face in duplicating experiments. See *The Golem: What Everyone Should Know about Science* (New York: Cambridge University Press, 1993).

31. For an account of the history of the Colorado, see Ivo Lucchitta, "The History of the Colorado River and the Grand Canyon," in *Grand Canyon Geology*, ed. Stanley S. Beus and Michael Morales (Flagstaff, Ariz.: Museum of Northern Arizona Press, 1990).

32. See Hayden White, "The Logic of Historical Narration," *Philosophy and History* 3 (1963): 4–14; D. L. Hull, "Central Subjects and Historical Narratives," *History and Theory* 14 (1976): 253–74.

33. On the role of prediction in the Earth sciences, see Naomi Oreskes, "Why Predict? Historical Perspectives on Prediction in Earth Science," in *Prediction: Science, Decision Making, and the Future of Nature*, ed. Daniel Sarewitz, Roger A. Pielke Jr., and Radford Byerly Jr. (Washington, D.C.: Island Press, 2000), pp. 23–40.

34. On the question of narrative and the historical sciences. See David Carr, *Time, Narrative, and History* (Bloomington: Indiana University Press, 1986), for an excellent summary and a set of references.

Notes 173

Chapter 6. The Philosophy of (Field) Science

1. A partial exception to this statement is K. S. Shrader-Frechette and E. D. McCoy, *Method in Ecology: Strategies for Conservation* (New York: Cambridge University Press, 1993).

2. The bare exception to this statement is with ethical questions surrounding the subjects of anthropological research.

3. Sources include Schumm, *To Interpret the Earth*, and field guides; David R. Olroyd, *The Highlands Controversy: Constructing Geological Knowledge through Fieldwork in Nineteenth Century Britain* (Chicago: University of Chicago Press, 1990); David Stoddard, "Darwin and the Seeing Eye," *Earth Science History* 134 (1994): 3–22; and Henrika Kohler and Robert E. Kohler, eds. "Science in the Field," *Osiris*, 11 (1996).

4. J. Von-Brakel. "On the Neglect of the Philosophy of Chemistry," *Foundations of Chemistry*, 1, no. 2 (1999): 111–74.

5. On the Green River Formation, see www.ucmp.berkeley.edu/tertiary/eoc/greenriver.html).

6. It remains to be seen how far the effects of global warming will take us toward greenhouse conditions. A complete melting of the Antarctic ice cap is thought impossible until plate tectonics move Antarctica away from the South Pole. From the long view of geologic history, we are still currently in an ice age, with the present interglacial period a slight summer thaw.

7. John Ruskin, *Elements of Drawing* (London: Dutton, Everyman's Library, 1907), p. 70.

8. Bruce V. Foltz, "Inhabitation and Orientation: Science Beyond Disenchantment," in Frodeman, *Earth Matters*.

9. Of course, other questions, such as the region's structure, could also have been investigated.

10. Charles Sanders Peirce, 1955.

11. Thomas Sebeok, 1989; quoted in John N. Deely, *Basics of Semiotics* (Bloomington: Indiana University Press, 1990).

12. Albert Borgmann, *Holding on to Reality: The Nature of Information at the Turn of the Century* (Chicago: University of Chicago Press, 1999), p. 17.

13. Barlow, 1989; quoted in Stoddart, *Darwin and the Seeing Eye*.

14. Alphonso Lingis, "Thinking in the Interrogative Mood," in *The Horizons of the Flesh: Critical Perspectives on the Thought of Merleau-Ponty*, ed. Garth Gillan (Carbondale: Southern Illinois University Press, 1973); Maurice Merleau-Ponty, *The Visible and the Invisible*, followed by working notes, ed. Claude Lefort, trans. Alphonso Lingis (Evanston, Ill: Northwestern University Press, 1968).

15. Polemarchus said, Socrates, you appear to have turned your face townward and to be going to leave us.

Not a bad guess, said I.

But you see how many we are? he said.

Surely.

You must either then prove yourselves the better men or stay here.

Why, is there not left, said I, the alternative of our persuading you that you ought to let us go? But *could* you persuade us, said he, if we refused to listen? (*Republic* 327c. trans with notes and an interpretive essay by Allen Bloom [New York: Basic Books, 1968], 3–4).

16. Don L. Eicher, Richard Dinar, Origin of the Cretaceous Bridge Creek cycles in the Western Interior, United States. In *Paleogeography, paleoclimatology, paleoecology*, 74, 1–2, pp. 127–146, 1989.

17. Maurice Merleau-Ponty, *Phenomenology of Perception*, trans. Colin Smith (London: Routledge and Kegan Paul, 1963), pp. 300ff.

18. Johnson, *Merleau-Ponty Aesthetics Reader,* p. 67.

19. Ibid., p. 65.

20. Martin Rudwick, *The Great Devonian Controversy: The Shaping of Scientific Knowledge among Gentlemanly Specialists* (Chicago: University of Chicago Press, 1985); Stuart McCook, "'It May Be Truth, But It Is Not Evidence': Paul du Chaillu and the Legitimization of Evidence in the Field Sciences," *Osiris* 11 (1996): 177–97.

Chapter 7. Being and Geologic Time

1. *Larry King Live*, 17 June 1997.

2. Roger Shattuck, *Forbidden Knowledge: From Prometheus to Pornography* (New York: St. Martin's Press, 1996).

3. Paul Saffo, Institute for the Future, quoted in *High Stakes in Cyberspace*, http://www.pbs.org/wgbh/pages/frontline/cyberspace/saffo.html.

4. There are two fascinating recent exceptions to this stance: Ted Kaczynski (aka the Unabomber), and Bill Joy, cofounder and chief scientist of Sun Microsystems. Kaczynski is dismissed as a psychopath; but the evil of his behavior shouldn't obscure the point that motivated his bomb making. As early as 1971, Kaczynski tried to create an organization to lobby for the restriction of federal funds for scientific research (see Alston Chase, "Harvard and the Making of the Unabomber," *Atlantic Monthly,* June 2000). Bill Joy raises serious questions concerning whether the combination of robotics, nanotechnology, and genetic engineering will create the conditions for the destruction of our species. See "Why the Future Doesn't Need Us," *Wired* 8.04, April 2000.

Notes 175

5. Nietzsche, *The Gay Science,* #125.

6. "Happiness, then, is not found in amusement; for it would be absurd if the end were amusement, and our lifelong amusements and sufferings aimed at amusing ourselves." Aristotle, *Nicomachean Ethics* 1176b30.

7. Cf. Gilles Deleuze and Félix Guattari, *Anti-Oedipus,* trans. Robert Hurley, Mark Seem, and Helen R. Lane (New York: Viking Press, 1977); and *A Thousand Plateaus: Capitalism and Schizophrenia,* trans. Brian Massumi (Minneapolis: University of Minnesota Press, 1987).

8. Cf. Lester Brown, *The State of the World* (San Francisco: Worldwatch Institute, 1997).

9. Styrofoam, properly called polystyrene, is a petroleum by-product that is used in a variety of products including plastic utensils and television sets.

10. Martin Heidegger, *Being and Time* (New York: Harper and Row, 1962), frontispiece (italics in the original).

11. Cf. Herbert Druyfus and Charles Spinosa, *Highway Bridges and Feasts: Heidegger and Borgmann on How to Affirm Technology,* at http://www.focusing.org/dreyfus.html.

12. Don L. Eicher, *Geologic Time* (Englewood Cliffs, N.J: Prentice-Hall, 1976).

13. John Locke, *Second Treatise of Government* (New York: New American Library, 1963), p. 334.

14. Albert Borgmann, *Crossing the Post-Modern Divide* (Chicago: University of Chicago Press, 1992).

15. For instance, see Steven Vogel, *Against Nature: The Concept of Nature in Critical Theory* (Albany: SUNY Press, 1996).

16. William Ophuls and A. Stephen Boyan Jr., *Ecology and the Politics of Scarcity Revisited* (New York: W. H. Freeman, 1992).

17. Ibid., p. 14.

18. Julian Simon, *The State of Humanity* (Cambridge: Blackwell, 1995), p. 25.

19. Ibid., p. 26. I owe the phrase "naked geologies" to Carl Mitcham.

20. Julian Simon, *The Ultimate Resource* (Princeton: Princeton University Press, 1981).

21. Mark Sagoff, "Do We Consume Too Much?" *Atlantic Monthly,* June 1997. Sagoff, however, draws quite different conclusions from Simon.

22. Theodore Roszak, *The Voice of the Earth: An Exploration of Ecopsychology* (New York: Simon & Schuster, 1992), p. 27.

23. For Shepard's argument, see *Nature and Madness* (San Francisco: Sierra Club Books, 1982).

24. Cf. http://www.nps.gov/planning/arch/verp.html.

25. Cf. Aristotle's *Ethics*, especially 1.3 and 6.1–7.

Chapter 8. Science and the Public Self

1. For information on the Georgia Basin Futures Project, see http://www.sdri. ubc.ca/GBFP/.

2. Nor is the danger entirely in the past. The Heritage Foundation, the most powerful conservative think tank in Washington, continues to call for the elimination of the Survey.

3. Article 1, section 8, clause 8.

4. A. Hunter Dupree, *Science in the Federal Government: A History of Policies and Activities to 1940* (Cambridge: Harvard University Press, 1957); Don K. Price, *Government and Science: Their Dynamic Relation in American Democracy* (New York: New York University Press, 1961); David Guston, *Between Politics and Science: Assuring the Integrity and Productivity of Research* (New York: Cambridge University, 2000).

5. The evolution of terms makes this point tricky to express: what is "conservative" in contemporary parlance is a variant of seventeenth-century political liberalism, which sought to ground sovereignty in the individual rather than the state. Indeed, as I discussed above (chapter 7) the views of both liberals and conservatives today are grounded in Lockean liberal political philosophy.

6. Mary C. Rabbitt, *Minerals, Lands, and Geology for the Common Defense and General Welfare* (Washington, D.C.: U.S. Government Printing Office, 1980), Vol. 1, p. 6. See also Rabbitt, *The United States Geological Survey, 1879–1989,* USGS Circular 1050 (Washington, D.C.: US Government Printing Office, 1989).

7. Cf. Wallace Stegner, *Beyond the Hundredth Meridian: John Wesley Powell and the Second Opening of the West* (New York: Penguin, 1954); Donald Worster, *A River Running West: The Life of John Wesley Powell* (New York: Oxford University Press, 2001).

8. Michael Sandel, *Democracy's Discontent* (Cambridge: Harvard University Press, 1996).

9. This is by convention—the ninety-eighth meridian lies more precisely along this line.

10. Cf. Rabbitt, *The United States Geological Survey,* p. 16. Criticizing the tendency to deify Powell, Karl Hess Jr. offers a revisionist account of Powell, laying many of the improper land management practices of the last one hundred years in the West at his feet: see "John Wesley Powell and the Unmaking of the West," in *The Next West: Public Lands, Community, and Economy in the American West,* ed. John A. Baden and Donald Snow (Washington, D.C.: Island Press, 1997). The standard for recent scholarship on Powell is Worster, *River Running West.*

11. This belief has prompted sharp rebuttals from some geologists. Granted, maps are the answers to a set of questions put to a landscape; when the questions change, so will the answers (and maps). Nonetheless, from the perspective of the originating legislation of the Survey, the task of mapping has largely been completed.

12. Cf. the American Academy for the Advancement of Science web page for current figures at: http://www.aaas.org/spp/dspp/rd/caprev00.htm#hi.

13. There is a large literature on this point: see, for instance, Shrader-Frechette and McCoy, *Method in Ecology.*

14. Monroe H. Freedman, "Professional Responsibility of the Criminal Defense Lawyer: The Three Hardest Questions," in *Ethics in Professional Life,* ed. Joan C. Callahan (New York: Oxford University Press, 1988), pp. 51–58.

15. http://www.usgs.gov/budget/stratplan.PDF.

16. For a brief discussion of scientific institutions as boundary organizations, see Guston, *Between Politics and Science.*

17. There is a remarkable variety of terms and disciplines that wrestle with the question of knowledge management. "Policy science" is a general term that includes such diverse areas as policy analysis, science policy, policy studies, information management, and decision support systems. Lasswell, the father of the policy sciences, has defined the policy sciences as fields that "study the process of deciding or choosing and evaluate the relevance of available knowledge for the solution of particular problems." Harold D. Lasswell, "Policy Sciences," in *International Encyclopedia of the Social Sciences* (New York: Macmillan, 1968), pp. 181–189.

18. I am indebted to Robert Harrap for this typology.

19. Case, in Gene Lessard, ed., *Decision Support Capabilities for Future Technology Requirements: Interagency Group on Decision Support* (IGDS), Washington, DC., 2001.

20. John Kelmelis, "The Changing Decision Environment," in *Report on the Decision Support Systems Workshop,* ed. Gene Lessard and Thomas Gunther (USGS Open file report 99-351), 1999, p. 5.

21. Ibid.

22. Information about these USGS programs can be found through searching the Survey's webpage at www.usgs.gov.

Chapter 9. Conclusion

1. W. Scott McLean, Eldridge M. Moores, and David M. Robertson, "Nature and Culture," in *Earth Matters: The Earth Sciences, Philosophy, and the Claims of Community,* ed Robert Frodeman (Upper Saddle River, N.J.: Prentice-Hall, 2000), pp. 141–150.

2. John Donne, *The Anniversaries,* ed Frank Manley (Baltimore: Johns Hopkins Press, 1963), p. 73–74.

The Sunne is lost, and th'earth, and non mans wit
Can well direct him, where to looke for it).
And freely men confesse, that this world's spent,
When in the Planets, and the Firmament
They seeks so many new; they see that this
Is crumbled out againe to his Atomis).
Tis all in pieces, all cohaerence gone;
All just supply, and all Relation:
Prince, Subject, Father, Sonne, are things forgot,
For euery man alone thinkes he hath got
To be a Phoenix, and that there can be
None of that kinde, of which he is, but hee.

3. Gary Snyder, Mountains and Rivers without End, (Washington, D.C.: Counterpoint, 1996), p. 145. Quoted in "Nature and Culture," op. cit., p. 148.

4. See http://www.uni-bielefeld.de/iwt/realworld/.

5. See http://www.mines.edu/newdirections.

6. See http://www.amdandart.org/.

INDEX

WITHDRAWN

JAN 2 4 2023

DAVID O. McKAY LIBRARY
BYU-IDAHO

PROPERTY
DAVID O. McKAY LIBRARY
BYU-IDAHO
REXBURG ID 83460-0